Kyoto City Travel Guide, Japan

Tourism information

Author
Caleb Gray.

SONITTEC PUBLISHING. All rights reserved. No part of this publication may be reproduced, distributed, or transmitted in any form or by any means, including photocopying, recording, or other electronic or mechanical methods, without the prior written permission of the publisher, except in the case of brief quotations embodied in critical reviews and certain other noncommercial uses permitted by copyright law. For permission requests, write to the publisher, addressed "Attention: Permissions Coordinator," at the address below.

Copyright © 2019 Sonittec Publishing
All Rights Reserved

First Printed: 2019.

Publisher:
SONITTEC LTD
College House, 2nd Floor
17 King Edwards Road,
Ruislip
London
HA4 7AE

Table of Content

SUMMARY **1**
KYOTO INTRODUCTION **5**
   Physical and Human Geography 6
      The landscape 7
         The city site 7
         Climate 8
         The city layout 8
THE PEOPLE **13**
   The economy 14
      Industry 14
      Commerce 15
      Transportation 16
   Cultural life 17
ADMINISTRATION AND SOCIAL CONDITIONS **20**
   Government 20
HISTORY **22**
TRAVEL **26**
   Tyoto Guide 29
      Districts 29
         Kyoto Central. 29
            Getting in 29
            Seeing 31
            Doing 40
            Buying 41
            Eating 43
            Drinking 50
            Sleeping 56
         Arashiyama 73
            Getting in 73
            Seeing 75
            Doing 89
            Buying 92
            Sleeping 94
         Higashiyama 96
            Getting in 97

Seeing	98
Doing	114
Buying	119
Eating	120
Drinking	123
Sleeping	124
Kyoto North	129
Getting in	129
Seeing	131
Doing	147
Buying	148
Eating	148
Drinking	151
Sleeping	152
Kyoto South	159
Getting in	159
Seeing	161
Doing	168
Buying	169
Eating	169
Drinking	171
Getting in to Kyoto	171
Getting around	184
Seeing	193
Doing	197
Buying	204
Eating	206
Drinking	210
Getting out	219
ATTRACTIONS	222
Enryaku-ji	222
Kiyomizu-dera	225
Fushimi Inari-Taisha	227
Chion-in	230
Tōfuku-ji	231
Gion	233
Nijō-jō	234

Daitoku-ji 236
Eikan-dō 237
Ginkaku-ji 238
Nanzen-ji 239
Tenryū-ji 240
Shōren-in 241
Kinkaku-ji 242
Aritsugu 243
Kanei 244
Giro Giro Hitoshina 244

Summary

The importance of travelling in our life?
Everyone has their very own reasons to travel. Some people travel for work, some travel for pleasure while for others it is just a way of life. They travel to live and to escape at the same time.

Whatever might be the reason to travel, here are few ways in which travelling would definitely change you and I think that is why travelling becomes so important in life:

Enjoy being alone: There is something therapeutic about being alone and being at peace with it. While you soak in a new culture, you also connect with your own inner self.

Learn to adapt: It is a different world out there, literally. Be it the pace of life, the language or simply the change in weather, it is always a change and you have to adapt to it. This is what makes travelling truly beautiful as you break away from the routine and adapt to something totally new.

Experience a new culture: Every place comes with its distinct cultural habits, you cannot think about New York without talking about its fast paced life and about Italy without enjoying its relaxed lifestyle. Similarly, while visiting the UK you might have to be a bit formal in your interactions with the locals, on the other hand, while greeting the people in Thailand, one can be really warm and casual.

Broaden your taste buds: Travelling without experiencing the local food is just not complete. It is not only a culinary experience but a cultural one as well.

Get out of comfort zone: From simple experiences like the weather, way of life or food to the more adventurous ones like trying a new sport, travelling really pushes ones boundaries to the core. You might end up participating in a street carnival in Brazil just like the locals or trying the local delicacies (read insects) in Thailand.

Indulge in Photography: It does not matter whether you are a professional or not. It is also irrelevant whether you have a DSLR or a very basic camera, while travelling what matters is the love and quest for seeing beautiful places and the sheer joy of capturing them in your lense. Travelling would in return give you your very own collection of amazing postcards of beautiful sunsets, snow laced mountains or sunny beaches.

Learn to escape: Travelling is the best way to break the routine. If you are in a bustling city, go ahead and experience the country life. If you are in a rural place, travel to a bustling city and experience its madness.

Stressed with the city life or work pressure? A spa break in Himalayas or Kerala is a must try.

Appreciate Nature: The quest to explore more when one is travelling always leads to a sense of amazement about nature. While most of us keep a track of technological advancements, Nature has its own ways of outshining all of these. The Antelope Canyon in Arizona or Turquoise Ice in Russia are the finest examples of this. For more, check out the most unbelievable places around the world.

Get closer to your own roots: While one travels and experiences a lot of different cultures and practices, it definitely brings one closer to his or her own roots. Travel helps one appreciate one's identity and culture.

Travelling is all about experiences. They can happen in terms of culture, people, places but most importantly with one's own self and this was all about

Kyoto Introduction

Kyōto, is a city, seat of Kyōto *fu* (urban prefecture), west-central Honshu island, Japan. It is located some 30 miles (50 km) northeast of the industrial city of Ōsaka and about the same distance from Nara, another ancient centre of Japanese culture. Gently sloping downward from north to south, the city averages 180 feet (55 metres) above sea level. Kyōto *fu* is at the centre of Kinki *chihō* (region). The city is one of the centres (with nearby Ōsaka and Kōbe) of the Keihanshin Industrial Zone, the second largest urban and industrial agglomeration in Japan.

The capital of Japan for more than 1,000 years (from 794 to 1868), Kyōto (literally, "Capital City") has been called a variety of names through the centuries Heian-kyō ("Capital of Peace and Tranquillity"), Miyako ("The Capital"), and Saikyō ("Western Capital"), its name after the Meiji Restoration (1868) when the imperial household moved to Tokyo. The contemporary phrase *sekai no Kyōto* ("the world's Kyōto") reflects the reception of Japanese culture abroad and Kyōto's own attempt to keep up with the times. Nevertheless, Kyōto is the centre of traditional Japanese culture and of Buddhism, as well as of fine textiles and other Japanese products. The deep feeling of the Japanese people for their culture and heritage is represented in their special relationship with Kyōto all Japanese try to go there at least once in their lives, with almost a third of the country's population visiting the city annually. Several of the historic temples and gardens of Kyōto were collectively added as a UNESCO World Heritage site in 1994. Area 320 square miles (828 square km). Pop. (2015) 1,475,183.

Physical and Human Geography

The landscape
The city site

Designated the site of a new capital by the emperor Kammu, Kyōto was laid out in 794 on the model of Chang'an (modern Xi'an), the capital of China's Tang dynasty. The plan called for a rectangular enclosure with a grid street pattern, 3.2 miles (5.1 km) north to south and 2.8 miles (4.5 km) east to west. The Imperial Palace, surrounded by government buildings, was in the city's north-central section. Following Chinese precedent, care was taken when the site was selected to protect the northern corners, from which, it was believed, evil spirits could gain access. Thus, Hiei-zan (Mount Hiei; 2,782 feet) to the northeast and Atago-yama (Mount Atago; 3,031 feet) to the northwest were considered natural guardians. Hiei-zan especially came to figure prominently between the 11th and 16th centuries, when warrior-monks from its Tendai Buddhist monastery complex frequently raided the city and influenced politics. The Kamo and Katsura rivers before joining the Yodo-gawa (Yodo River) to the south were, respectively, the original eastern and western boundaries. But the attraction of the eastern hills kept the city from filling out to its original western border until after World War II. Kyōto is actually cradled in a saucer of hills on three sides that opens to the southwest toward Ōsaka.

Climate

Kyōto is most beautiful in spring and fall. The rainy season (June–July) lasts three to four weeks; summers are hot and humid. Winter brings two or three light snows and a penetrating "chilling from below" (*sokobie*). The yearly mean temperature of Kyōto is about 59 °F (15 °C); the highest monthly mean, 80 °F (27 °C), is in August, and the lowest, 38 °F (3 °C), is in January. The average yearly rainfall is about 62 inches (1,574 millimetres).

The city layout

The original grid pattern of the streets has been retained. Numbered avenues run east and west, Shijō-dōri ("Fourth Street") being the busiest. Karasumadōri, running north from the Japanese National Railways station, divides the city roughly into halves. Under it is one of the two lines of the municipal subway. The other, newer line, completed in 1997, runs from the JR Nijō station in the west across the city to the east and then to Daigo, southeast of the city. Kyōto was the first city in Japan to have electric streetcars (starting in 1895), which eventually made it necessary to widen the major thoroughfares to allow for citywide service.

The historic area of Kyōto has few large factories or businesses, a fact reflected in the look of the inner city shops and workshops, residences, and offices all standing side by side. Stringent building codes limit the height of buildings in order to preserve the overall look of the historic city. Characteristic of the architecture are tiled roofs and wood weathered to dark brown, but telephone poles (now made of concrete) and a forest of television antennas protrude at every turn. A typical Kyōto house presents a narrow and low front to the street, but as it recedes it gains in height and embellishment all this a reflection of its past history and character: wariness of the marauding monk, the zealous revenue collector, or the curious neighbour. Rarely does one enter a home beyond the front vestibule; if one is invited in, it is good form to demur.

Because of earthquakes and conflagrations, the attacks of monks from Mount Hiei, and the Ōnin War (1467–77), which utterly destroyed the city, little of Kyōto's historical architecture predates the 17th century. Replacements and renovations, of course, followed previous plans, but the single shining example of Heian-period architecture remaining is the soaring Hōō-dō ("Phoenix Hall") of the Byōdō-in (Byōdō Temple), located a few miles southeast of the city on the banks of Uji River (Uji-gawa).

Buddhist temples and Shintō shrines abound. Their grounds and those of the Kyōto Imperial Palace (Kyōto Gosho) and Nijō Castle (Nijō-jo) give Kyōto more green areas than most Japanese cities. Kyōto claims some

1,660 Buddhist temples, more than 400 Shintō shrines, and even some 90 Christian churches. Major Buddhist institutions include East Hongan Temple (Higashi Hongan-ji) and West Hongan Temple (Nishi Hongan-ji), the former with the world's largest wooden roof of its kind and the latter containing some of the best examples of architectural and artistic expression of the Azuchi-Momoyama period (1574–1600); Ryōan Temple (Ryōan-ji), with its famous rock-and-sand garden; Tenryū Temple (Tenryū-ji), in the Arashiyama district to the west; Kiyomizu Temple (Kiyomizu-dera), built on stilts on the side of the eastern hills; and Kinkaku Temple (Kinkaku-ji), the Golden Pavilion, burned down by a deranged student in 1950 but rebuilt exactly, and Ginkaku Temple (Ginkaku-ji), the Silver Pavilion, both of which were products of the Ashikaga shoguns' attraction to Zen. The great Shintō shrines are Kitano, Yasaka, and Heian, the last built in 1894 to commemorate the 1,100th anniversary of Kyōto's founding.

The buildings of the Kyōto Imperial Palace, originally located farther west, date from 1855 and are re-creations, in the same monumental Japanese style, of earlier structures that were destroyed by fire. Nijō-jo, built by the Tokugawa shogunate, is a "token" castle, but it contains many cultural treasures; it is known for its "chirping floors" (to signal the approach of an intruder) and elaborate wall paintings of the Kanō school. The two foremost examples of traditional Japanese landscape architecture are the Katsura Imperial Villa (Katsura Rikyū) in the southwest corner of the city and the Shūgakuin Rikyū set in the northeast hills. Katsura underwent a complete renovation using perfectly matched modern materials; its buildings are models of Japanese architectural aestheticexpression. Shūgakuin contains three gardens, the third with an artificial lake. From there one can view the entire expanse of the city stretching out to the south.

The people

Kyōto is one of the largest cities in Japan. Its population which includes a sizable foreign community comprising mainly Koreans (many brought there forcibly during World War II), Chinese, and Americans has remained relatively stable for a number of years. Most of the city's residents live in the central districts, but increasingly people are moving to outlying and suburban areas.

A major item remaining on the municipal agenda has been how to assimilate the thousands of *burakumin,* the historical outcaste group, who live in segregated communities in the city. This has been a continuing social problem largely in the older urban areas of western Japan, particularly Kyōto, Ōsaka, and Kōbe.

Despite the fact that the last discriminatory legal bars were removed in 1969, social and occupational progress has lagged.

The economy

Industry

Kyōto is a city of thousands of medium and small industries, many of them family owned and operated. Traditional handicrafts abound, and their manufacture for the tourist trade is an important element of Kyōto's economic life. The central part of the city is crowded with small workshops, which produce such typical Japanese goods as fans, dolls, Buddhist altar fittings, and lacquer ware. Antipollution measures have forced the once-thriving Kiyomizu pottery kilns to move to nearby Yamashina.

For centuries silk weaving, centred in the north-central Nishijin district, has been one of Kyōto's major industries. Along with the geisha and entertainment sector, the fine textiles, delicate fabrics, and embroidery represent a continuity of Kyōto's traditional role as the centre of Japanese culture. In addition, the Fushimi district in southern Kyōto, favoured with excellent water, produces some of Japan's finest sake. Also located in southern Kyōto are several industries established after World War II that produce industrial ceramics, women's garments, and medical instruments. Since the early 1980s, companies such as Kyocera Corporation (originally Kyōto Ceramics Co., Ltd.) have put Kyōto in the forefront of such high-technology industries as electronics, robotics, and computers. Throughout the 1990s and into the early 21st century, however, the city, like the rest of Japan, struggled with economic recession.

Commerce

Kyōto is mainly a consumer city. It is the national centre of silk and fine textile wholesaling, but its main commercial activity is retail trade. The Gion and Pontocho districts, famed for their geisha and *maiko* (apprentice geisha), offer a variety of traditional and foreign food and drink. During the summer, *yuka* (platforms on stilts) are set up on the banks of the Kamo River in the heart of town, and strolling troubadours pass below as a reminder of how Kabuki theatre originated. Traditional Japanese inns (*ryōkan*) abound, and many Western-style hotels cater to the wedding, tourist, and convention trades. A large conference centre near the foot of Mount Hiei hosts major industrial exhibitions and international conferences.

Transportation

Most of Japan's east–west traffic must come through Kyōto. During the Tokugawa period(1603–1867) the city was the western terminus of the Tōkaidō, the road that connected Kyōto to Edo (now Tokyo). River traffic to Ōsaka favoured the Yodo. Today the numerous high-speed bullet trains of the Shinkansen give reliable service to major cities east and west. Interurban lines between Kyōto and Ōsaka–Kōbe and Nara provide fast and frequent local service. Kyōto itself finally abandoned streetcars in the 1970s. The Meishin Expressway links Kyōto to Ōsaka and Nagoya.

Cultural life

During the millennium that Kyōto served as the nation's capital and residence of the imperial family, it became the preserver of the Japanese "spirit." This is exemplified in its varied and unique cultural institutions: the schools of tea ceremony (*cha-no-yu*) and flower arranging (*ikebana*); the theatrical arts of Noh, Kabuki, and traditional dance; or the masterpieces of calligraphy, painting, sculpture, and architecture that can be found everywhere in the city. Kyōto is the repository of hundreds of designated "national treasures" and "important cultural objects," representing a significant proportion of the national total. Included among these are individuals who have been named "living national treasures" (*ningen kokuhō*) in recognition of their superior skills in the traditional arts and crafts.

Most of the important works of art are housed in Kyōto's temples and shrines, many of which are themselves listed as national treasures. Even institutions that do not normally display their collections periodically have public showings at which their treasures can be viewed. Kyōto also has numerous museums, including Kyōto National Museum (founded 1889), containing national treasures; Kyōto Municipal Museum of Art (1933); and Kyōto Municipal Traditional Crafts Centre (1976).

The birthplace of traditional Japanese drama, Kyōto maintains an active theatrical life. Several Noh stages offer frequent performances, and the annual opening performance (*kaomise*) at the Minami Theatre is the customary inauguration of the national Kabuki season. A traditional form of humorous pantomime, *Mibu kyōgen*, is performed faithfully by troupes of amateurs.

The three major festivals (*matsuri*) Aoi in May, Gion in July, and Jidai in October are almost national events. The Jidai-matsuri ("Festival of the Ages") is a parade depicting, in period costume, Japan's entire history. The Gion-matsuri (Gion Festival) dates from the 9th century and features more than 30 elaborate, carefully preserved, hand-drawn floats, some decorated with French Gobelin tapestries imported through Nagasaki during Tokugawa times. The northern hills Mount Hiei with its scenic drive and the Takao district for its fall foliage are famed for their well-tended stands of Japanese cedar (*sugi*).

Administration and social conditions

Government

Kyōto urban prefecture, which extends to the Sea of Japan, is under the administration of an elected governor, while the city is administered by an elected mayor and city council.

Education

Kyōto was traditionally organized into extended neighbourhoods, called *machi*, and after the Meiji Restoration these were designated as the administrative units for general public education; in this way, the city preceded the national effort to systematize primary education. Kyōto is surpassed only by Tokyo in its number of institutions of higher learning, but it claims several more Nobel Prize laureates than Tokyo, a point it reminds the latter of from time to time. The city's relatively calm atmosphere, its distance from the hurly-burly of national government, and its numerous cultural and religious institutions and facilities are cited as prime reasons for its educational advantages. There are more than 40 two-year and four-year colleges and universities with a total annual enrollment of more than 100,000 students. The state-run Kyōto University, established in 1897, is the second most prestigious school in the country. Dōshisha University, the leading private educational institution, was founded in 1875 by Niijima Jō (also called Joseph Hardy Neesima), who was the first Japanese to graduate from a Western college (Amherst College in 1870). Major Buddhist universities include Ryūkoku, Ōtani, and the smaller Hanazono.

History

Kyōto as the national capital dates from 794, although the area was settled earlier by Korean immigrants who brought with them the skills of sericulture and silk weaving. As noted above, the planned city was between the Katsura and Kamo rivers, but it soon extended beyond the eastern banks of the Kamo. The powerful Fujiwara familydominated the Heian period. Excessive Buddhist influence at the old capital of Nara had occasioned the removal of the government to Nagaoka and then to Kyōto, where the building of Buddhist temples was proscribed. As an exception, Rashōmon, the great southern gateway, was flanked by Tō-ji on the east and Sai-ji on the west; Sai-ji was short-lived, but the handsome, five-tiered pagoda of Tō-ji is a classic landmark.

Following the decline of the Fujiwara and the ascendance of the Minamoto in the late 12th century, political and military leadership was vested in a shogun ("generalissimo"), the first of whom, Minamoto Yoritomo, chose to administer the expanding domains from Kamakura to the east. It was during the Kamakura period (1192–1333) that many of the Buddhist temples were established, and indigenous sects of Buddhism, together with Zen from the continent, appeared. During the ensuing Muromachi period (1338–1573), the Ashikaga shogunate moved the government back to Kyōto. The aristocratic culture of the Heian era blended with the culture of Zen that had developed under the samurai (warriors), resulting in the refinement of the Nō theatre, the tea ceremony and flower arranging, and pottery making.

By the mid-16th century, however, the city had been so devastated that St. Francis Xavier, on a pilgrimage to

Kyōto, could not even locate the Imperial court, much less seek an Imperial audience. The city's fortunes revived under the regimes of the national unifiers Oda Nobunaga and Toyotomi Hideyoshi. Buddhists, especially the Tendai monks on Hiei-zan, were such an anathema to Nobunaga that he set fire to the entire monastery complex; but under Hideyoshi, an ardent patron of the arts, Kyōto flourished. One of his tea parties was attended by thousands of people and went on for days.

With the ascendance of the Tokugawa shogunate at the beginning of the 17th century, the political centre again moved, this time to Edo (modern Tokyo). The Imperial court was left to pursue its ceremonial functions, and access to it was carefully monitored. Only after the arrival of Matthew Perry in 1853 and the collapse of the Tokugawa did Kyōto again come to the fore. At the Nijō-jo in 1867 the last Tokugawa shogun finally turned back to the Imperial court his mandate to rule the nation, marking the first time in more than 200 years that a ruling Tokugawa had set foot in Kyōto.

Shortly after the proclamation of the Meiji Restoration, however, the young Meiji emperor took up residence in the new capital, Tokyo a move that has not been forgotten in Kyōto. Kyōto busied itself in outbidding Ōsaka to become in 1872 the site of an annual exhibition that was held for more than 30 years. During World War II U.S. Secretary of War Henry L. Stimson, recalling his visits to Kyōto, struck the city from the list of targets for aerial bombing. Its cultural treasures intact, it maintains a special place in the hearts of the Japanese and, increasingly, in the eyes of the world.

Travel

Kyoto is old Japan writ large: atmospheric temples, sublime gardens, traditional teahouses and geisha scurrying to secret liaisons.

Japan's Spiritual Heart
This is a city of some 2000 temples and shrines: a city of true masterpieces of religious architecture, such as the retina-burning splendour of Kinkaku-ji (the famed Golden Pavilion) and the cavernous expanse of Higashi Hongan-ji. It's where robed monks shuffle between temple buildings, prayer chants resonate through stunning Zen gardens, and the faithful meditate on tatami-mat floors. Even as the modern city buzzes and shifts all around, a waft of burning incense, or the sight of a bright vermillion *torii* gate marking a shrine

entrance, are regular reminders that Kyoto remains the spiritual heart of Japan.

A Trip for the Tastebuds
Few cities of this size pack such a punch when it comes to their culinary cred, and at its heart is Nishiki Market ('Kyoto's kitchen'). Kyoto is crammed with everything from Michelin-starred restaurants, chic cocktail bars, cool cafes and sushi spots to food halls, *izakaya* (Japanese pub-eateries), craft-beer bars and old-school noodle joints. Splurge on the impossibly refined cuisine known as *kaiseki* while gazing over your private garden, taste the most delicate tempura in a traditional building, slurp down steaming bowls of ramen elbow-to-elbow with locals, then slip into a sugar coma from a towering *matcha* (powdered green tea) sundae.

A City of Artisans
While the rest of Japan has adopted modernity with abandon, the old ways are still clinging on in Kyoto. With its roots as the cultural capital of the country, it's no surprise that many traditional arts and crafts are

kept alive by artisans from generation to generation. Wander the streets downtown, through historic Gion and past *machiya* (traditional Japanese townhouses) in the Nishijin textile district to find ancient speciality shops from tofu sellers, *washi* (Japanese handmade paper) and tea merchants, to exquisite lacquerware, handcrafted copper *chazutsu* (tea canisters) and indigo-dyed *noren* (hanging curtains).

Cultural Encounters
If you don't know your *matcha* (powdered green tea) from your *manga* (Japanese comic), have never slept on a futon or had a bath with naked strangers, then it doesn't matter as this is *the*place to immerse yourself in the intricacies of Japanese culture. Whether you watch *matcha* being whisked in a traditional tea ceremony, spend the night in a ryokan, get your gear off and soak in an onsen, join a raucous *hanami* (cherry-blossom viewing) party or discover the art of Japanese cooking you'll come away one step closer to understanding the unique Japanese way of life.

Tyoto Guide
Districts

Though dwarfed in size by other major Japanese cities, Kyoto is vast in terms of its rich cultural heritage - the material endowment of over a thousand years as the country's imperial capital. The city's numerous palaces, shrines, temples and other landmarks are spread out over the following districts:

Kyoto Central.

Central Kyoto encompasses the urban heart of Japan's former imperial capital. From the carefully tended gardens and stately buildings of the Imperial Palace in the north to the massive, ultra-modern showpiece structure of Kyoto Station in the south, this district has a bit of everything that makes Kyoto what it is today: a marbled mix of old and new, of immeasurably ancient traditions and fast-paced modernity.

Getting in

Kyoto's extensive rail, subway, and bus networks can all be accessed through the city's main transportation hub: the gargantuan glass-and-steel structure of Kyoto Station .

By train
Kyoto Station is a major stop on the Tōkaidō Shinkansen Line. From the station, travellers arriving by shinkansen (or by other railway lines) can easily access the city's municipal subway and bus systems.

By subway
Central Kyoto is served by two intersecting subway lines. The north-south Karasuma Line (which stops at Kyoto Station) and the west-east Tōzai Line link up at Karasuma-Oike Station near the city centre.

By bus
Several important bus routes (covering not only Central Kyoto but other parts of the city as well) start and end at the Kyōto-eki-mae terminal - which, as the name indicates, is right in front of Kyoto Station. Take the station's Karasuma/North exit and you'll see the bus

terminal, which is divided into four boarding platforms (from A to D) and has signs in English identifying key stops on each route. For detailed route information, pick up a copy of the helpful "Bus Navi" leaflet from the information centre near the terminal.

Seeing

Nijō Castle, (Nearest bus stop: Nijojo-mae. Nearest subway station: Nijojo-mae). Open daily, 8.45am-5pm, with last admission at 4pm. Certainly one of the highlights of Kyoto, with fine gardens and splendid centuries-old structures. The castle was originally built by the Tokugawa shoguns to serve as the shogun's residence in Kyoto. The series of ornately-decorated reception rooms within the Ninomaru Palace complex is particularly impressive, and known for its "nightingale floors" - wooden flooring which makes bird-like squeaking sounds when stepped on so as to give advance warning when someone was approaching. From the empty base of the donjon that once overlooked the innermost section of the fortress (known as the Honmaru), you can get good views over parts of the castle compound and the wider city beyond.

Nijo Jinya, (Just south of Nijo Castle). This former (and still inhabited) samurai house offers a look into how people used to live. The guided tour focuses on the measures taken to avoid and deal with the risk of fire and attack, with several trap doors and escape routes, along with some innovative anti-conflagration architecture. However, it's not a cheap tour and no photos are allowed. Moreover, tours were suspended for two years from the end of 2009 Golden Week (May) while repairs are carried out. You also may be turned away if you don't speak Japanese. Tour ¥1,000.

The Museum of Kyoto, (Located on Takakura-dori. Nearest bus stop: Shijo Karasuma. Nearest subway station: Karasuma Oike). Open daily 10am-8.30pm. The museum features many ancient artifacts. It may be particularly worthwhile if you have an interest in ancient pottery. It is undergoing rennovations from

New Years and will reopen in July 2011. Admission ¥500.

Kyoto International Manga Museum , (1-minute walk north from the Karasuma Oike subway station),. Open 10 AM to 6 PM (last admission 5:30 PM); closed on Wednesdays - or the following Thursday if Wednesday is a national holiday - and during the New Year holidays (as well as during regular maintenance periods). Housed in an old elementary school building, the museum holds over 300,000 manga-related items ranging from rare Meiji-era publications to the works of contemporary artists.

One of its main attractions is the so-called "Wall of Manga": a vast collection of some 50,000 volumes arranged on shelves running along the building's corridors. Much of the collection is in Japanese, but there is a sizeable selection of manga translated into various foreign languages (including English) on the ground floor. Visitors are welcome to pick out and read anything they choose from the "Wall of Manga" (although the books can't be checked out for offsite reading), which explains the large numbers of children and young adults that throng the museum - and the large Astroturf field just outside - during opening hours. The museum also hosts special temporary exhibitions and other manga-related events. Admission ¥800 adults, ¥300 high-school students, ¥100 elementary school students; special exhibits cost extra.

Nishi Honganji, (*15 minute walk northwest from Kyoto Station*), 075-371-5181. Open from 6 AM to 5 PM. One of Kyoto's World Heritage Sites, the current building dates back to the 1600s. It is the head temple of the Honganji sect of the Buddhist Jodo sect. Entrance is free.

Higashi Honganji, (*5 minute walk north from Kyoto Station*), 075-371-9210. The majestic main hall of Higashi Honganji, said to be the largest wooden structure in the world, can accommodate up to 5,000 people and is the headquarter of the Shinju Sect of Buddhism. The "hair rope" is perhaps the most interesting site in the temple, as it is just that; an extremely thick rope made mostly from human hair. Entrance is free.

Shosei-en Garden, (*Two blocks east of Higashi Hongan-ji Temple*) 075-371-9210. Also known as Kikoku-tei, Shosei-en Garden was commissioned by Prince Minamoto no Toru. He created the Ingetsu Pond was designed to look like the Shiogama coast in Miyagi Prefecture. During the Tokugawa Period the garden was given to Higashi Hongan-ji Temple, restoring the old sections and adding on to the garden.

Cherry blossoms at Tō-ji Temple
Tō-ji Temple. Open 9 AM to 5:30 PM. Although its famed for its pagoda, the tallest in Japan, the other structures within the complex are equally impressive with surprisingly colorful interiors and a variety of precious Buddhist sculptures on display. The rest of the temple grounds are made up of a relaxing garden, with many cherry blossoms in the spring. It is also famous for its flea markets, held on the 21st of every month.

Entrance fee: ¥500 (special exhibitions have separate fees).

<u>Kyoto Tower</u>, (*Just north of Kyoto Station*). Open from 9 AM to 9 PM. A sightseeing tower that provides views of Kyoto's urban sprawl. Entrance fee: ¥700.

<u>Bukkoji Temple</u>, Shinkai-cho Shimogyo-ku, 075-341-3321. A temple of Shin Buddhism established by Shinran.

<u>Mibudera Temple</u>, 075-841-3381. 8 AM to 5:30 PM. This temple is most famous for its Setsubun celebration, particularly for the Mibu Kyogen performances on February second and third. During normal times, the temple and the garden/mound are not particularly exciting. The treasures housed are interesting and cheap to see. It is free to walk around the temple grounds, but the garden and treasures each cost ¥100 to see.

<u>Shinsen-en Garden</u>, 167 Monzen-cho, Nakagyo-ku, 075-821-1466. Open from 9 AM to 10 PM. Although

cherry blossom-viewing and festivals can be seen all over Japan today, Shinsen-en Garden is where the very first organized cherry blossom viewing festival took place. Admission is free.

<u>Umekoji Steam Locomotive Museum</u>, Kankiji-cho, Shimogyo-ku (*10-min walk from Tanbaguchi, 20-minute walk from Kyoto Station*), 075-314-2996. 9:30 AM-4:30 PM. This former locomotive depot preserves 19 steam locomotives. At the center of the museum is a 20-track roundhouse surrounding a turntable that houses and exhibits the preserved locomotives. The roundhouse is an Important Cultural Property designated by the government of Japan as the oldest reinforced concrete-made car shed extant in Japan. There is also a short exhibition operation track to operate trains. A steam train locomotive operates three times a day and makes a round trip on the track in about 10 minutes. ¥400 for entrance, additional ¥200 for steam train ride.

File: GEAR longrun Kyoto.png

GEAR (*GEAR Kyoto*), 56 Benkeiishicho, Nakagyo-ku, Kyoto City 1928 build. 3F (*On Sanjo street between Teramachi and Gokoumachi*), 075-254-6520. 10:00~19:00. GEAR is a non-verbal theatre show that performs in Kyoto and incorporates elements of technology, skilled performance art. It is the first long-run show with original content in Japan. GEAR is contemporary non-verbal entertainment that combines a superb cast and high technology to tell a story for all humankind about the power of touch. Set in a broken toy factory in the future, robot workers encounter a doll that comes to life and takes them on a journey to discover their humanity... ¥3700.

Imperial Park
The Imperial Park is a large, peaceful area in the centre of Kyoto, centred around the Imperial Palace. The Palaces are only open to visitors on free guided tours, and bookings must be made at the Imperial Household Agency, online or in their office to the west of the palace complex.If you're in Kyoto for an extended

amount of time, the park can make for a very pleasant afternoon, and it's large enough to let you forget the noise of the city outside the walls. It's home to 50,000 trees, including cherry, plum and peach tree orchards (mostly in the northern section).

Kyoto Imperial Palace, (*A 5-10 minute walk south from the Imadegawa subway station, Karasuma subway line*). For the specific Imperial Palace, English tours at 10am and 2pm Mon-Fri (by appointment only) Tours of the other palaces take place at other times. The Palace is a reconstruction (dating from 1855), though the Emperor doesn't actually spend much time there, *and* the guided tour doesn't actually enter the Palace buildings, only peeking at them from the outside, but nevertheless, it provides interesting insight into the lives of the Imperial Court and it's the only Imperial site in Kyoto that offers English guides. Show up an hour before the tour at the Imperial Household Agency building (west of Kyoto Imperial Palace), and they'll let you join if there's space, or make a booking for another day if there isn't. If you don't want to chance it, advance bookings can also be made online through the Imperial Household Agency's official site. Entrance is free.

Sentō Imperial Palace. Located within the grounds of Kyoto's Imperial Park, the Sento Imperial Palace is arguably the most competitive for reservations, because this is the palace where the present Imperial family stays when in Kyoto.

Doing

Nishijin Textile Center, Horikawa-Imadegawa, 075-451-9231. While visitors may just go to the museum to see the history of Nishijin Textiles, you may also want to try dressing up as a geisha or trying your hand at weaving. You need reservations for each activity, and separate fees are charged for each activity. Weaving costs ¥1800 adult (¥1500 for students) and dressing up as a geisha costs ¥10000.

Kyoto Butoh-kan (*Butoh-kan*), Tsukinukecho 135, Nakagyoku, Kyoto 604-8202 (*Just west of Karasuma Oike Subway stop*), 075-254-6520. Thursdays 6pm / 8pm. In the heart of the city is located the Butoh-kan, the world's first theatre devoted to weekly performances of the elusive dance of Butoh. Performances are by world famous Butoh dancer Tenko Ima, every Thursday at 6pm and 8pm. She is accompanied by live Shamisen music. The "theatre" is actually an ancient plaster storehouse, so the atmosphere is vivid and intimate, because there are only eight seats per show. 3000.

Buying

The city's main shopping district is centered on the intersection of Shijō-dōri and Kawaramachi-dōri, a short distance from the Kamo River and a manageable walk away from the neighbouring Gion district in Higashiyama. Kawaramachi Station on the Hankyū Line puts you right in the heart of the action, within easy reach of three major department stores and a wide assortment of other shopping options.

For electronics, head up to Teramachi and turn left; for clothes boutiques, including your chance at finding the *perfect* Engrish t-shirt, turn right into the covered arcade portion of Teramachi and Shinkyōgoku, which runs parallel.

Specific places worth checking out include the following:
Toji Flea Market. On the 21st of each month, Toji hosts a large flea market on and around the temple grounds. It's like a one-day festival, with long rows of food vendors joining an odd assortment of sellers everything from elegant Japanese crafts and rare plants to piles of old postcards, photos, movie posters, and appliances from decades past.

Gallery Gado 27 Miyashiki-cho Hirano, Kitaku (*on Kinukake no Michi, near Kinkakuji*). 075-464-1655. Open everyday, 10:00 AM to 6:00 PM. Gallery Gado sells modern woodblock prints (*ukiyo-e*) with traditional themes. The gallery also has catalogs of the work of artists who are maintaining this art form. All prints are authentic woodblock prints; postcard-sized prints are available for ¥800, medium-sized prints for ¥2000-3000, and large prints for a few ten thousand yen.

Junkudo (*8th floor of BAL building on Kawaramachi-dori between Shijo and Sanjo streets*). +81 075-253-6460. Open daily 11 AM to 8 PM. Huge bookstore with big selection of English books and magazines.

Eating
Budget
Musashi Sushi one of the oldest kaitenzushiya (conveyor belt sushi) restaurants in Kyoto, it is located directly across chain Kappa Sushi at the corner of Sanjo/Kawaramachi. All of the sushi is handmade, though it may take a while to see something new float by. Fortunately, the seats surround the chefs, so you can request whatever you want if you don't see

something you like. Price: ¥137 per plate (usually 2 pieces per plate).

Kappa Sushi is a chain kaitenzushiya (conveyor belt sushi) restaurant on the corner of Sanjo and Kawaramachi at the entrance to the Shinkyogoku/Teramachi covered mall. Lots of variety and cheap prices, but the sushi isn't handmade machines are used to cut the rice and fish. Price: ¥100 per plate (usually 2 pieces per plate).

Mr. Young Men is a pleasantly grubby okonomiyaki restaurant downtown, at the corner of Shijo and the covered shopping street of Teramachi. Basic English menus are available. A basic dish of Osaka-style okonomiyaki will run about ¥800, although a few variations (including a bizarre cheese and potato version) are available for about the same price.

Hati Hati is an Indonesian restaurant on Kiyamachi, near Takoyakushi. It has great food and atmosphere, but it's occasionally converted into a bar and a performance space for local bands and DJs at night on weekends. For really late night food on Kiyamachi, there is cheap, open-air falafel cafe a couple doors down from Hati Hati that never seems to close.

Donguri is a cheap yet very nice okonomiyaki restaurant on the Northwest corner of Kawaramachi and Shijo. It's a sub-level place so it might take a bit to find it. It is next to the Excelsior Coffee; if you walk past The Body Shop you went too far. It's about ¥500 for an okonomiyaki and about ¥300-500 for a namachuu (mid sized mug of beer). Expect to pay ¥800-900 in the evening. Great place for a date or nicer evening.

Mid-range

Arash's Kitchen, Shōgoin Sannōchō, 4 O Its right across from Kyoto University Hospital`s main entrance, 075-751-5177. Open from 11:30 AM to 10:00 PM. Everyday.. Iranian Restaurant that opened in Feb 2013. Owner is Iranian and works alone. Great place for persian food but also sells falafel and other middle eastern dishes. Lunch menu is from ¥800-1200 range in price. Dinner is from ¥1000-1800, the portion sizes are large.

<u>Kappa Sushi</u> (on Pontocho) is a reasonably-priced (for fresh sushi) restaurant. They have an English menu which is, unfortunately, inferior to the Japanese menu. Specials change daily, but are generally on the pricey side. Sit at the sushi bar, and eat well-apportioned nigiri off of banana leaves with your fingers. Not a bad place to try real o-toro for ¥800 a plate.

<u>efish</u> 798-1 Nishihashizume-cho +81 075-361-3069 (*near the Idemetsu gas station, across the river from Keihan Gogo station*. Open every day, 11 AM to 11 PM (until 10 PM in the winter). This cafe, tucked away down a hidden side street, has a trendy ambiance and river views. For lunch, try the okra curry (¥850) or soup and bread set (¥650)

<u>Shishin Samurai Cafe & Bar</u>, 230-1 Kamimyoukakuji-cho Nakagyo-ku, (075) 231-5155, proclaims that an increase of food production, food self-sufficiency, and

the decrease of food waste can prevent war. This cafe serves local Japanese foods as much as possible to increase food self-sufficiency and sustainability. In addition this cafe uses 5% of its gross sales to aid homeless people and orphans who are suffering from a lack of food. Furthermore, this cafe aims to reintroduce declining Japanese traditional customs and keep these traditions   alive. Also, this cafe plans to hold lectures, discussions and forums concerning peace and food sustainability. Open Wednesday to Monday 12:00 to 23:00 (please, note different menu items during cafe and bar times).

Siam A tiny but wonderful Thai curry restaurant on Marutamachi-dori about 100m east of Nishioji-dori. The food is delicious, reasonably priced and spice levels are indicated on the menu. Relax in a soft-lit room decorated with exotic paintings from Bali, while the friendly staff prepare your meal right in front of you. English menu available. Open: 11:30-15:30 & 18:00-21:00. Closed: Wednesdays.

Fuka Located west of the Imperial Palace and just a bit south of the Kyoto Prefectural Office, this old shop makes the best nama-fu (wheat gluten filled with sweet bean paste) in Kyoto and s upplies many sweet shops and restaurants throughout the city. There might not be enough supplies to sell over the counter, so it is best to arrive early. Open: 9AM-5PM. Closed: Mondays

Tengu A chain izakaya offering their own beer and good shared food with occasional seasonal specials. One is located underground with an entrance near the corner of Sanjo/Kawaramachi.

Anil A nice Nepalese restaurant in the Daini Kankou building 6th floor on Kiyamachi. It's got a great atmosphere and awesome food. The dahl, cheese nan and momo dumplings are highly recommended.

Torikizoku. 5 or 6 pm to late. Torikizoku is the most popular yakitori chain in Kansai. There are several locations in Kyoto - most convenient for travellers is in Kawaramachi/Shijo, just before the bridge, or between sanjo and shijo, on kiyachou-dori. The yakitori is delicious, comes in generous serves and is very cheap. It's very popular with both locals and expats, and is always busy. Try to come before 7:30 to secure seats. Look for the Japanese characters on the distinctive yellow and red sign. All food/drink ¥300 each.

Splurge
Pontochō is a narrow lane running from Shijo-dori to Sanjo-dori, one block west of the Kamo River. One of Kyoto's most traditional nightlife districts, the restaurants here run the gamut for super-exclusive geisha houses to common yakitori bars. Many have pleasant open-air riverside terraces. Rule of thumb is, any establishment with a menu and prices outside is OK, but others are best skipped.

Mishima-tei: If you have a yearning for *sukiyaki*, and your pockets are deep, you must visit Mishima-tei at the junction of Teramachi-dori and Sanjo-dori. Here you will be bowed in and shown to your own private tatami room by your personal kimono-clad hostess.

There, having helped you to order, she will prepare your *sukiyaki* feast on the hotplate set between you. Order the "premium beef", and the richly marbled meat will just melt in your mouth, and require almost no chewing whatsoever: it is delectable and it should be since two of you will spend around ¥25,000 in less than an hour on 360 grams of beef and a few vegetables! (For the cost-shy, there is a 'tourist set' on the menu which results in a bill of about ¥13,600 for 2.)

Drinking

Zen Cafe. A place to meet travelers and locals as it is located next to popular hostel "K's House". The staff are friendly and speak good English and are happy to offer advice on what to see and do from a local's point of view. ¥390 per drink (Spirits, basic cocktails and draught beer) and bar snacks.

Bar This Way. Open from 7 PM to 1 AM (close at 3 AM on Fri. & Sat.). A Dutch-owned bar located next to Royal Hotel (between Kawaramachi Sanjo and Oike dori). They offer a large selection of beers especially from The Netherlands and Belgium and many other drinks and food (including handmade gyozasoup). The staff speaking Dutch, English, Japanese, Chinese and German are friendly and prices very reasonable. Bar This Way is on the 3rd Floor (Tanakabld.) and you need to use the elevator to get in. Dutch beer sells for ¥650, gyoza for ¥700.

Ing. No night in Kyoto is complete without the requisite after hours visit to all-night Ing (a.k.a., "Box Bar," or "the office"). Proprietor Hako-san will keep bringing you the booze, and he's happy to join you for a drink when offered. Food there is always an option - tofu salad & potato pizza are good for the price (¥600). Get ready for Rolling Stones, competitive Jenga, sharing tables with odd drunk people, and clothes permanently soaked in smoke. Good luck finding it. If you see Hamid's Falafel you're on the right track. Ing is on the second floor of a building slightly south of Hamid's. Sapporo sells at ¥600 each shareable bottle.

<u>Sake Bar Yoramu</u>, Nijo-dori east of Karasuma (*Marutamachi and Karasuma-Oike subway stations*), +81-75-213-1512. 6 pm - 12 am, closed Mondays and first Sunday of the month. From the unusual to the standard, this sake bar has both an impressive selection of traditional Japanese rice wine. Even more impressive is the barkeep and owner, who's from Israel, who can translate your preferences in wine into sake. Well-aged sake is available, busting the myth that sake does not age. Traditionally-brewed sake ranging from slightly cloudy to yogurt-like may also be available.

<u>Nikki's Bar</u>, Nishi-Kiyamachi 804 Daini Kankou Building. 20:00-05:00 daily. This is a nice little bar ran by a gregarious Nepalese guy named Nikki. It's got a great bunch of regulars and new customers are always warmly welcomed. It's located just north of Hamid's Kebab shop. Mixed drinks and beer run ¥700 per drink and shots are ¥500. It's a little hard to find because it's

on the 8th floor. If you can't find it ask the folks working at Hamid's. ¥700

Sugar Trip, 448-13 Shimokajii-cho Kawaramachi-Imadegawa (*On Imadegawa-dori a few blocks south of the intersection* with *O*), 075-211-1145. A ritsy cocktail bar with a variety of drinks from the standard beers to champaigne and cava. Most people come for one of the many cocktail varieties that this bar is famous for. Original cocktails sell for ¥700-750, Smoothie cocktails for ¥900, Beer for ¥650-700, tonic ¥700.

Rub-a-Dub, Tsujita bld.BF,115 Ishiya-cho, Kiyamachi-Sanjo, 075-256-3122. A one-room Jamaican Reggae bar. It can either be an over-crowded mess or a box of delirious fun, depending on which record is on (and how much you like Red Stripe) either way you must try the jerk chicken. Must be 18 years or older to enter. Jerk chicken, fried rice, and chicken curry each for ¥600.

A bar, 075-213-2129. A-bar, a hard-to-find (on 2nd floor) izakaya close to the Shijo/Kiyamachi corners, makes a great start to the evening. Food is good and reasonable - daily sashimi specials and fried goods, especially. You share long tables with foreigners and locals alike; a friendly thing to do would be to pour beers for your neighbors and Suei-san, the proprietor. ¥550 Yebisu.

Pub Africa, KyotoRokkaku Terrace Bld 1F, 075-255 4518. Although many think this is an Africa-themed bar, there is nothing very African about it. If there's a football match from home that you need to catch, they'll show it here, and they have cheap Asahi jugs. Beers half off during Happy Hour. Also, their fooseball table is very well kept. Across from the Hub, infra.

Bungalow, shijo horikawa higashiiru (*at the intersection between Shijo street and samegai street, near horikawastreet and omiya station*),0752568205. 15:00-26:00 (!?). Nice, hip but cozy, place with craft beers on 10 taps, organic wines and some barfood (bread, cheese, lamb etc.). When we went there it was their 2nd anniversary which they celebrated by offering 10 kinds of IPA on tap. Recognizable from the street by it's plastic walls.

British and Irish Pubs
The Hub: on the small streets connecting Kiyamachi to Kawaramachi, lots of TVs for sports, cheap beer (¥700/pint) (especially with a ¥500 membership) and more expensive imports; food, however, is mediocre. This is basically the headquarters for English-speaking tourists and gaijin residents for happy hour. Happy hour (5-7 pm) discounts cocktails only. If you want some inside information about where to go, where to eat, what to see, etc., ask a group here. One of the larger bars in Kyoto, it is a popular spot for happy hours and goodbye parties. The real draw is the foosball, darts tournaments, and, upstairs in the back, the pool table.

Hill of Tara: a quiet Irish-style pub with good food. A bit more expensive than the frozen stuff from the Pig or the Hub, but a much mellower scene. In the Spring and Summer, they have a nice, though small, second floor balcony.

<u>McLoughlin's</u>: Is presided over by the most amiable owner/chef Tadg McLoughlin (formerly of Tadg's Irish Pub), located on Kiyamachi between Sanjo and Nijo. Food is reasonably priced, with main course starting at ¥1,200 and a 5 course special menu which is great value. Great quality beers, domestic and foreign (including microbrews). The staff are friendly and speak English. Live music on weekends. Giant screen TV (Mr McLoughlin being a Rugby fanatic), darts, foosball and a great view of east Kyoto. Happy hour is 5pm-8pm. Name changed to Tadg's in summer 2010.

Sleeping

The great majority of Kyoto's accommodations can be found here. Staying closer to Kyoto Station provides immediate access to the Shinkansen and the hub of the city bus network; closer to Karasuma-Oike puts you in the midst of downtown and closer to the Gion. They're only minutes apart by subway, making the choice merely a matter of personal convenience.

Budget

Hostels

Guesthouse Yahata, 544 Yahata-cho, Gojo-agaru, Nishinotoin, Shimogyo-ku (*off Gojo-dori, west of the subway station*), +81 (0)75-204-5897 (Japanese only). checkin: 4-9 PM; checkout: 11 AM. Bunk beds from ¥2500, private rooms from ¥8000 (2-4 people), with free breakfast.

JAM Hostel, Tokiwacho170 Higashiyama (*At the corner of Gion-Shijo station at the Keihan line*),+81-752013374,. checkin: 3-10 PM; checkout: 12 PM. Dorms from ¥2100, laundry, fast and free wi-fi, common area with bar.

J-Hoppers Kyoto Guesthouse, 51-2, Nakagoryo-cho, Higashikujo, Minami-ku (*8 min. walk south from Kyoto Station, near Kujo subway station*), +81 (0)75-681-2282, SKYPE: jhoppers, checkin: 3-10 PM; checkout: 8-

11 AM. A new and clean backpackers hostel. Rental bikes ¥500/day, Internet ¥300/hour. No curfew; up-to-date local information by native staff. Dormitory bed ¥2500.

K's House Kyoto, 418 Nayacho, Shichijo-agaru, Dotemachi-dori, Shimogyo-ku (*9 min. walk east from JR Kyoto Station along Shichijo-dori, 4 min. walk from Keihan Line Shichijo Station*), +81 (0)75-342-2444, fax: +81 (0)75-342-2440). checkin: 3-10 PM; checkout: 11 AM. Opened in November 2003, this clean, foreigner-friendly hostel with English speaking staff has amenities like internet access and kitchens. The hostel itself can be difficult to find, as it is located down a narrow street off the main road. Dormitory room ¥2500, twin/double/triple room from ¥2900, single room from ¥3500 (prices per person).

Khaosan Kyoto Guesthouse, 568 Nakanocho, Bukkoji-agaru, Teramachi-dori, Shimogyo-ku (*1 min. walk south from Hankyu-line Kawaramachi Station, exit 10*), +81 (0)75-201-4063. checkin: 3–9 PM; checkout: 8–11 AM.

Opened November 2010. Staff are very friendly and they provide heaps of local information. No curfew, free (but somewhat slow) Wi-Fi access, free tea and coffee available at Japanese style living room. 10 beds Dorm room, ¥2000; 6 beds Mix(female) Dorm ¥2200; Twin (Double bed)Private room ¥5600(2 person); 4 beds mix dorm, ¥2500.

<u>Kyoto Capsule Ryokan</u>, 204 Tsuchihashicho, Shimogyo-ku (*7 min. walk northwest from Kyoto Station*) +81 (0)80-3113-6960. checkin: 16:00–21:30; checkout: 10:30. A capsule-style hotel catering to international budget travelers. Operated by the same people as Tour Club Kyoto.¥3500/person singles, ¥3990/person doubles.

<u>Kyoto Cheapest Inn</u> (Hostel Kyotokko), 783 Sabamatsu-cho, Marutamachi Omiya-Dori, Kamigyo-ku. (At the south-east of the cross road named Marutamachi Matsuyacho. Near Nijo Castle, 1-3 min. walk from bus stop Horikawa Marutamachi, 7 min. walk northeast from JR Nijo station), +81 (0)75-821-3323. Credit cards

accepted, English available, sheets included. Free wifi, computer use. Long stay discount. Additional charges for various services - use of printer or fax, changing sheets more frequently, etc. Bike rental (¥500/day) Dorms from ¥2200–2500, private rooms, ¥7800. Discounts common in winter.

<u>Sandal Wood Hostel</u>, 2F 32-2 Ttakada-Cho ,Saiin, Ukyou-ku (*Bus from JR Kyoto Station, right in front of the Daikokuya Super Market. 5 minute walk to the Saiin Metro Station*), +81 (0)75-585-7052. checkin: 12:00. New hostel with friendly, English-speaking staff. Guests are always greeted with an unlimited amount of either ice cold water, hot coffee, or iced coffee. It is not uncommon for the hosts to offer plates of fruits and nuts during nights in. Free WiFi, towel use, washer and dryer, common room, left luggage service, and much more. Air-conditioned dorms are of ¥2700 per night.

<u>Tomato Guesthouse</u>, 135 Shimizu, Nishi-iru Shiokoji-Horikawa, Shimogyou-ku (*7 min. walk west from Kyoto*

Station), +81 (0)75-203-8228. checkin: 4-9 PM. Dorm ¥2200, private singles ¥3600–3900.

Tour Club, 362 Momijicho, Higashinakasuji, Shomensagaru, Shimogyo-ku (*9 min. walk northwest from Kyoto Station*), +81 (0)75-353-6968. A friendly, clean hostel with both dorm and private rooms. There is a beautiful zen garden and traditional Japanese-living room with a small library of local travel information. Free wifi, coffee and tea and the chance to try on a kimono. Air-con, bicycle rental, coin operated internet terminals and laundry are also available. Double en-suite ¥3490 per person, quad en-suite ¥2,930 per person, dorm beds ¥2450 per person.

Uronza Guesthouse, 427 Yohoji-cho Shimogyo-ku, 075-341-3226. checkin: 6 am; checkout: 11 AM. A guesthouse offering Japanese and Western-style rooms. Online reservations are currently unavailabed to make reservations via phone or e-mail (staff not likely to speak English). Prices start at ¥2200.

Hotels, minshuku & ryokan

<u>Budget Inn</u>, (*near Nishi-Honganji, 7 min. walk northwest from Kyoto Station*),+81 (0)75-344-1510. checkin: 4:00–9:30 PM; checkout: 10:30 AM. Under the same management as Tour Club (above). A variety of dorm and private rooms, with elevator access. Kitchen and laundry facilities available. Offers discounts for stays beyond 4 nights. Dorm bed ¥2500/night, private rooms ¥10,980 triple through ¥14,980 quad.

<u>Crossroads</u>, 45-14 Ebisu Banba-cho, Shimogyo-ku (*20 min. walk west of Kyoto Station, or #205 bus to Ume Koji Koen-mae then 2 min. walk northwest*), +81 (0)75-354-3066 (fax: +81 (0)75-354-3022). checkin: 4 PM; checkout: 10 AM. A ryokan with shared shower & toilet facilities. 11 PM curfew. Three rooms: one person ¥4000, two persons ¥7350, three persons ¥10,400.

<u>Econo Inn Discount Hotel</u>, 67 Hirai-cho, Kawaramachi-Gojo Sagaru, Shimogyo-ku (*15 min. walk northwest from Kyoto Station, or just south of Kawaramachi-Gojo stop on buses 4, 17, 205*), +81 (0)75-343-6660 (fax: +81

(0)75-343-6667). checkin: 3 PM–11 PM; checkout: 11 AM. 21 Western-style private rooms: singles, doubles, and triples. All rooms have a bath unit, air-conditioner and TV. Caters more to long-term stays. Sliding rate scale depending on length of stay: singles go from ¥5880 for one night down to ¥3880 for 21 nights or more; a few small short-term singles range start at ¥3780.

<u>Hotel Iida</u>, 717 Shiokoji-agaru, Akezu-dori, Shimogyo-ku (*3 min. northeast of Kyoto Station*), +81 (0)75-341-3256 (fax: +81 (0)75-351-3051). Mostly Japanese style rooms, with a few Western rooms, both varieties with or without private bath. Singles ¥5250–7875 (Japanese), ¥6300–7875 (Western); doubles ¥8400–14,700; triples ¥12,600-23,625.

<u>Ikoi-no-Ie</u>, 885 Ushitora-cho, Rokujo-dori, Shinmachi Higashi-iru, Shimogyo-ku (*12-15 min. walk northwest from Kyoto Station, 5 min. west from Gojo subway station*), +81 (0)75-354-8081 (fax: +81 (0)75-354-8068). checkin: by arrangement; checkout: 11 AM. New

facility, opened 2007. All non-smoking rooms, some en-suite. The ground floor rooms near the lobby can be noisy. LAN ports in most rooms. Singles with shared bath ¥4750, private bath ¥7600; doubles ¥7600–8400 shared, ¥9600–11,000 private; triples ¥9600 shared, ¥12,000–13,500 private; quad ¥15,000 private.

<u>Palace Side Hotel</u>, Karasuma Shimodachiuri Agaru, Kamigyo-ku (*3 min. walk north from Marutamachi subway station K07*), +81 (0)75-415-8887(fax: +81 (0)75-415-8889). checkin: 2 PM; checkout: 11 AM. It's exactly where the name suggests: across the street from the Kyoto Imperial Palace and park, on Karasuma (near the intersection with Marutamachi). It's a Western-style hotel reminiscent of a much more expensive hotel that could use a good scrubbing. The staff speak fluent English, and the front desk is always open, as are computers with Internet access in the lobby. It's often used by academic groups from nearby universities, though, so advance reservations should be made. There are discounts for stays of three or more

nights.Singles ¥6000–7000, twin ¥9000–9800, doubles ¥9800.

Ryokan Hiraiwa, 314 Hayao-cho, Kaminokuchi-agaru, Ninomiyacho-dori, Shimogyo-ku (*15 min. walk northeast from Kyoto Station, or take buses #17 or #205 from pier A2 to Kawaramachi-Shomen, the third stop*), +81 (0)75-351-6748. A self-proclaimed ryokan (really a minshuku) catering almost entirely to the foreign market, in an old Japanese house plastered with English signs, warnings and tips. All rooms are Japanese style. Traditional breakfast is available for an extra charge. Shared bathrooms or a public bath half a block away. But it's cheap and reasonably friendly, though opinions beyond that vary widely. Slightly inconveniently located halfway between the station and the center of town (it's bit of a hike to either).Singles ¥4200–5250, doubles ¥8400.

Ryokan Kyoraku, 231 Kogawa-cho, Shichijo-agaru, Akezu-dori, Shimogyo-ku (*6 min. walk north from Kyoto Station*), +81 (0)75-371-7161 (fax: +81 (0)75-371-1260).

checkin: 3–10 PM; checkout: 10 AM. Recently renovated, with 14 Japanese-style rooms (half with private bath, half without) and two Western-style double rooms (both with private bath). 11 PM curfew. Singles ¥5200–6000 with shared bath, ¥6000–6600 private; doubles ¥9200–10,200 shared, ¥11,000–12,300 private; triples ¥13,800–15,200 shared, ¥16,000–17,700 private.

Ryokan Yuhara, 188 Kagiyacho, Shomen-agaru, Kiyamachi-dori, Shimogyo-ku (*15 min. walk northeast from Kyoto Station*), +81 (0)75-371-9583(fax: +81 (0)75-371-9580). checkin: 3 PM; checkout: 10 AM. Japanese style rooms, shared bath, sink in room. Recently renovated, very nice rooms, very clean, very friendly. 11 PM curfew. Singles/doubles/triples ¥5,250/9,660/14,490 per room with shared bath, no meals included.

Station Ryokan Seiki, 24-5, Kitakarasuma-cho, Higashikujo, Minami-ku (*5 min. walk south from Kyoto Station*) +81 (0)75-682-0444 (fax: +81 (0)75-682-0171).

Shabby building, but the staff is friendly. Singles ¥5500, doubles ¥8000–9000, triples ¥12,000–13,000.

Super Hotel Kyoto Karasuma Gojo, Karasuma Dori, Gojo Kudaru, Osaka Machi 396-3 (*10 min. walk from Kyoto Station, or at exit 8 of Gojo subway station*) +81 (0)75-343-9000 (fax: +81 (0)75-343-9001). checkin: 3 PM–midnight; checkout: 10 AM. A Japanese budget hotel chain. All rates include tax and breakfast. Singles ¥6090 (¥5040 off season, ¥7140 peak season); doubles ¥7140–8180–9240.

Toyoko Inn Kyoto Gojo-Karasuma, 393, Gojo-Karasumasho Karasuma-dori Matsubara-sagaru Shimogyo-ku (*15 min. walk north from Kyoto Station, 3 min. walk from Gojo subway station, exit 2*), +81 (0)75-344-1045 (fax: +81 (0)75-344-1047), checkin: 4 PM; checkout: 10 AM. A Japanese budget hotel chain. Good value for twin rooms. Online reservations showing vacancies & bookings available on all sites, enter as "General Guest" if you do not have membership. Two other locations nearby, at Shijo-Omiya and Shijo-

Karasuma, with similar prices. Singles ¥6200, doubles ¥7200, triples ¥8200.

Midrange
Gimmond Hotel (*2 min. walk east from Karasuma-Oike subway station*), Takakura-Oike-dori, Nakagyo-ku, +81 (0)75-221-4111 (fax: +81 (0)75-221-8250). checkin: 1 PM; checkout: 11 AM. A foreigner-friendly hotel, neat and tidy and located downtown near City Hall. Discount for Internet booking. Including taxes and fees: Singles ¥9,586–10,741, doubles ¥16,170, twin rooms ¥16,747–23,100.

Hearton Hotel Kyoto, Higashi no Toin Dori Oike Agaru, Nakagyo-ku (*2 min. northeast of Karasuma-Oike subway station, exit 1*),+81 (0)75-222-1300 (fax: +81 (0)75-222-1313). checkin: 2 PM; checkout: noon. Mid range, Western-style hotel located downtown. Single ¥11,000, twin ¥22,400.

Hotel Monterey Kyoto, 3 Jyo Minami Karasuma-dori, Nakagyo-ku (*West side of Karusuma, south of Sanjo*), +81 (0)75-251-7111. checkin: 2 PM; checkout: 11 AM.

Opened in March 2007. The staff are very keen to please. 15 minute stroll to Sanjo Shopping Arcade and less than five minute walk from subway station. Rates vary but they have discounts for internet booking and travel agents offer combined JR tickets and room rates. Includes spa and two restaurants (French and Japanese). Singles around ¥15,000–18,000, doubles around ¥20,000–23,000.

Hotel Sugicho, 172 Moriyamacho, Oike-agaru, Tominokoji, Nakagyo-ku (*5 min. walk east from Karasuma-Oike subway station*), +81 (0)75-241-0106, fax: +81 (0)75-221-7271),. checkin: 4 PM; checkout: 10 AM. Mostly Japanese-style rooms, with a few Western. Breakfast and dinner available. Adjacent to Kyoto Gyoen and the Nishiki Markets. Standard plan around ¥9,450–¥18,900, Limited plan around ¥3,900–77,350.

Kyoto Garden Hotel, Muromachi-dori, Oike Minamiiru, Nakagyo-ku (*About 1 min. west of Karasuma-Oike subway station (Karasuma subway line), exit 4-1*), +81 (0)75-255-2000 , fax: +81 (0)75-255-2389). checkin: 3

PM; checkout: 10 AM. Convenient downtown location; a short walk away from the Kyoto International Manga Museum, a long (but manageable) walk away from Nijo Castle. All rooms are non-smoking. Guests with their own LAN-enabled laptops/netbooks can get internet access in their rooms free of charge; just borrow a connection kit from the front desk. Actual rates vary depending on the time of year and discounts/special offers are available for online bookings. Single ¥9240, double ¥12,600–13,650, twin ¥14,700–16,800, triple ¥19,950.

<u>Kyoto Tower Hotel</u>, Karasuma-dori Shichijo-sagaru, Shimogyo-ku (*1 min. walk north from JR Kyoto Station, immediately across the street*), +81 (0)75-361-3212 (fax: +81 (0)75-343-5645). checkin: 1 PM; checkout: 11 AM. Foreigner-friendly hotel, and the location across the street from JR Kyoto Station is impossible to miss. The same company operates two additional hotels nearby: the Kyoto Tower Hotel Annex, a few blocks northwest, and the Kyoto Dai-Ni Tower Hotel, east of

the station. Kyoto Tower: Singles ¥8,000–14,500, twin ¥16,000–31,000. Annex and Dai-Ni: ¥6,500–11,500, twin ¥14,000–19,800.

Ryokan Shimizu, 644 Wakamiya Agaru Shichijo, Shimogyo-ku (*5 min. walk northwest from Kyoto Station, near Nishi-Honganji*), +81 (0)75-371-5538 (fax: +81 (0)75-371-5539). A modern style ryokan which is welcoming to foreign visitors. The owners can speak some English. En-suite facilities are provided but no meals are available. There is a communal Japanese bath facility. ¥6,000/person (¥5,000 during winter), higher near holidays.

Citadines Karasuma-Gojo Kyoto, 432 Matsuya-cho Gojo-dori Karasuma- Higashiiru Shimogyo-ku Kyoto 600 8105, 81-75 352 8900. Enjoy the comfort and convenience of a apart'hotel that offers exclusive living spaces replete with modern facilities and home comforts.

Splurge

<u>Kyoto Hotel Okura</u>, Kawaramachi-Oike, Nakagyo-ku (*at Kyoto Shiyakusho-mae subway station, T12*), +81 (0)75-211-5111 (fax: +81 (0)75-254-2529). checkin: 1 PM; checkout: 11 AM. A large, modern Western-style hotel located downtown. ¥19,000 for a single, through ¥49,000 for a double-occupancy corner room; top-floor suites climb higher still.

<u>New Miyako Hotel</u>, 17 Nishikujo-Inmachi, Minami-ku (*across street from Kyoto Station, Hachijo exit*), +81 (0)75-661-7111 (fax: +81 (0)75-661-7135). checkin: 1 PM; checkout: 11 AM. The largest hotel in Kyoto with over 700 rooms, and the prices to match. Located immediately south of Kyoto station. If you get a room facing north, you'll be able to see the bullet trains coming in and out of the station, as well as the glass windows from the exterior of the Isetan department store that seem to reflect the sky if the weather conditions are just right. The new and slightly more expensive south wing opened in late September of

2005. ¥11,550 singles, ¥21,000 doubles, ¥57,750 suites, tax included.

Arashiyama

Arashiyama is located in Kyoto. While this western part of the city is dismissed in most Western guidebooks in a brief paragraph suggesting "other attractions", the area is rightfully very popular with Japanese tourists and well worth a visit.

Getting in
By train
Local trains of the Sagano Line (San'in Main Line) depart from Kyoto Station and stop at three stations in the northwest part of the city, including Saga Arashiyama (a good starting point for exploring the Arashiyama area). Note that express services may not stop at the stations you need to disembark at, so it's usually best to rely on local trains.

The Matsuo area is served by the Hankyū Arashiyama Line, which branches off from the Hankyū Kyōto Main Line at Katsura Station.

The Randen tram line, Kyoto's only surviving streetcar, ends at Arashiyama Station, directly in the heart of the area. The main line runs from the central city at Shijo-Omiya, while the Kitano branch line travels to Hakubaicho, serving several sites in the northern city. Fare is a flat ¥200, and an all-day pass is ¥500.

By subway
Although the municipal subway system doesn't serve Arashiyama directly, travellers coming from other parts of the city (especially Central and Higashiyama) can use the Tōzai Line as far west as Nijō Station, where they can transfer to JR trains running on the Sagano Line (San'in Main Line).

By bus
Bus 11, 28, and 93 will get you to the Arashiyama area. The 91 Bus will take you to Daikaku-ji. The Matsuo area can also be reached using Bus 28, and it's the only bus

that travels to this area from Kyoto Station. Be aware that the ¥500 Bus Pass does not work for any of the Arashiyama or Matsuo-bound buses and you will be required to pay the ¥220 fare from the pass boundary.

From march 22nd 2014 the one day bus pass *'DOES'* include the Arashiyama area.

Seeing

Togetsukyō Bridge. This picturesque bridge spans the Hozu River, which usually has at least a bit of water in it.

Tenryū-ji, 68 Saga Tenryuji Susukinobaba-cho (*Main entrance near the busy Togetsukyō Bridge intersection*), 075-881-1235. Open from 8:30am-5:30pm Mar-Oct, to 5pm Nov-Feb. One of the city's UNESCO World Heritage Sites and the main temple of the Rinzai sect of Buddhism in Kyoto; it's also considered one of Kyoto's Five Great Zen Temples. Tenryu-ji was founded in 1334, but the current buildings all date from the last century: pleasant, but unremarkable. However, there is a lovely garden and pond, designed by the Zen master Musō Soseki, that is worth a look - and well worth taking a leisurely stroll around. Plus, you can see much of the temple from the garden with the garden-only ticket. After your walk, head out the back way and through the splendid bamboo forest to reach the Ōkōchi Sansō villa (see below). Admission is ¥500 for just the garden, or ¥800 for the garden plus temple.

Ōkōchi Sansō, (*Near the bamboo grove behind Tenryū-ji*), 075-872-2233. 9 AM to 5 PM. A splendid mountain retreat, previously occupied by Japanese silent screen legend Ōkōchi Denjirō. The grounds have something beautiful to offer each season but are probably at their best during autumn, when the trees explode into fiery shades of red and gold. Take a long, leisurely walk through the villa's beautiful gardens and savour the fine views of the city below. There is a small museum on the grounds dedicated to the former owner's life and work. Entrance is ¥ 1000; the price includes a cup of "matcha" (green tea) and a small dessert in the villa's teahouse.

<u>Nonomiya Shrine</u>, 075-871-1972. Open from 9 AM to 5 PM. A small shrine located amidst Arashiyama's famous bamboo forest. It was here that women were once trained prior to becoming shrine maidens at Ise Shrine, the holiest Shinto Shrine in Japan. Entrance is free.

<u>Iwatayama Monkey Park</u>. A great place for those looking to get away from the abundance of temples and shrines in the city, feeding the macaque monkeys atop the mountain is worth the entrance fee (and the demanding climb!). Don't bring food up with you, though - peanuts are on sale inside the shack on top of the mountains, and the monkeys are well aware of it. There's a pond next to the shack, and the monkeys seem particularly fond of the keeper's motorcycle, which is usually parked there. There's a ¥550 admission fee to enter the park; peanuts cost extra, but you know the monkeys appreciate it.

<u>19th Century Hall</u>, (*Just outside Saga Arashiyama station*). A museum covering the unlikely combination of steam locomotives and pianos. Probably best to look at it from the outside, and listen to the amusing tinny music it blasts out.

<u>Otagi Nenbutsu-ji Temple</u>, 2-5 Fukatani-cho (*By bus, take #72 from Kyoto station to Otagidera-Mae, or within Arashiyama, catch #62 or #72.*) 075-865-1231. Open from 8:00 AM to 5:00 PM. Despite being omitted from virtually all guidebooks, it's one of the true unknown gems of Kyoto. It was founded in the eighth century, and went through an unlucky patch for a millennium or so; by turns it was destroyed by flood, fire and typhoon, and had to move location a few times. Today, it sits a short distance from the end of Saga Toriimoto, one of Kyoto's three historic preservation districts.

Two fierce statues guard the entrance. Once you're through the gate, though, you'll find over 1200 small (knee-to-waist high) statues, each with its own unique character - you'll see a cheerful boxer near the entrance, but you could spend hours checking out the rest, and you'll do it in relative seclusion, since this is well away from the tourist trail. The statues were carved in 1981 by amateurs under the direction of master sculptor Kocho Nishimura. Moss and forest have begun to reclaim the area, and if you've ever wondered what Angkor Wat would look like crossed with Japanese *kawaii*, this is your chance. Admission is ¥300.

Daikakuji Temple, 4 Saga-Osawa-cho. While it is a temple today, originally, it was the villa of Emperor Saga. It is well-known by those who practice *Ikebana*, the Japanese art of flower arranging, as it is the birthplace of Saga Goryu, a school of Ikebana. Often, there are examples of Saga Goryu near the entrance to the temple. The temple itself is reasonably large, with some artwork inside. The view of the Osawanoike Pond is quite relaxing. Admission are ¥500 for Adults, ¥300 for Students. ¥200 for pond.

Adashino Nenbutsu-ji, 075-861-2221. Open 9 AM to 4:30 PM. The famous Priest Kukai established this temple for the purpose of saying prayers for Arashiyama's dead. The temple grounds are filled with approximately 8000 Buddhist statues, each representing an unknown or forgotten person. Although it is famous for its statues, just like Otagi Nenbutsu-ji, Adashino Nenbutsu-ji is a spiritual place and a graveyard, so it has greater historical and spiritual significance, as well as impressive and beautiful. If you take a walk through the small bamboo-lined path to the upper area, you'll find actual grave sites instead of the statues in the lower area. There is also an area similar to the purification spots found at most temples however, at this one, you are supposed to pour water on each of the statues as you walk around it. This is a form of reverence and worship, and the Japanese who enter (particularly those who come to the upper area) come to pray, so while it may be fun, try also to be respectful.

Gioji Temple, 075-861-3574. Open from 9 AM to 5 PM. Mentioned in the Tales of Heike, this is the site where sisters Gio and Ginyo come to devote their lives to Buddhism. Although the temple itself is rather small, the visit is made worthwhile by its vivid bright green moss garden, and those unwilling or unable to visit the moss garden of Kokedera (see below) may find a fair substitute here. Please note that the moss is at its best from June to autumn. Entrance fee: ¥300.

Takiguchi-dera Temple, (*Located on the same road as Gioji, at the end*). A quiet, peaceful temple of less interest than nearby Gioji Temple.

Jojakkoji Temple, 075-861-0435,. Open 9 AM to 5 PM. This temple is quite beautiful in the autumn when the leaves are changing, and the view of the city from just above the pagoda is a truly spectacular. Entrance is ¥400.

Nison-in Temple. A large temple complex that houses two ancient sculptures of Buddha; one of Shakamuni

Buddha and the other of Amida Buddha. It also houses the graves of some famous Japanese people. Unless you have interest in visiting one of the graves, the complex seems expensive compared to other temples of the same price with much more interesting sites and history. Admission is ¥500.

<u>Hokyo-in</u>. Home to the graves of the court's former enemies, as well as a beautiful moss garden.

<u>Seiryo-ji</u> (*sagashaka-do*). This is the former home of Toru Minamoto who is believed to be the man that the famous Tale of Genji's protagonist Genji was inspired by.

<u>Horinji Temple</u>. One of the five head Shingon temples in Kyoto. The Boddhisatva Akasagarbha is enshrined in this temple. The complex offers a nice view of Kyoto City. The lights here are quite beautiful during the autumn Kyoto Light-Up.

<u>Senko-ji</u> (*Daihikaku*). This temple was built as a memorial temple for those who died while working on

dams and other projects under Suminokura Ryoi. There are a variety of monuments and statues on the temple grounds, and a haiku from the famous poet Matsuo Bassho was written about the cherry blossoms on the temple grounds. The walk along the Hozu River leading to the temple is arguably more enjoyable than the temple itself, as the water often displays quite vivid blues and greens.

Koryuji Temple, 32 Hachiokacho, 075-861-1461. Open from 9 AM to 5 PM. Of all the temples in Kyoto, Koryuji is the oldest, dating back to the 12th century. It also houses the Miroku Bosatsu, the first item in the nation to be designated a National Treasure. Entrance fee: ¥700.

Tōei Movie Village, 10 Uzumasa Higashihachioka-cho. A unique park in Kyoto featuring movie sets from a variety of famous Japanese television shows, which visitors can explore. Demonstrations, performances, and on-sight filming are all part of the experience.

Inside, you can see costumes from famous children's shows.

Matsuo area

Located just south of Arashiyama, the Matsuo area is rarely mentioned in most guidebooks however, it does have a few interesting sites, particularly Kokedera, a World Heritage Site and Matsuo Taisha which the area is named after.

<u>Matsuo Taisha</u>, 075-871-5016. Shrine open from 5 AM to 6 PM. Treasure house open from 9 AM to 4 PM. A shrine that's rarely visited by foreigners, Matsuo Taisha is a popular place for sake brewers to pray. The shrine existed prior to the establishment of Kyoto as Japan's capital and later received offerings from the Heian court. The shrine is famous for its water, said to be pure, as well as its interesting gardens and landscape.Shrine is free, ¥500 to see shrine treasures and garden area.

Katsura Imperial Villa, (About 15-20 minutes on foot from Katsura Station on the Hankyū Kyōto Main Line, 5-8 minutes on foot from Katsura Rikyū-mae bus stop). A real cultural treasure, renowned for its magnificent gardens and fine classical architecture. You can obtain permission to join a tour of the property either through the Imperial Household Agency's official site (which also contains a detailed list of instructions or by applying in person at the agency's Kyoto office (near the Imperial Palace). Be sure to apply well in advance of your visit: slots are extremely limited and the much sought-after online permits are rationed out through a lottery selection process.

Umenomiya Shrine. This shrine is oddly dedicated to gods of both easy delivery and sake, because it is believed that the goddess Saketokekono was so delighted at the birth of her son that she made and drank sake. In addition, the stone to the right (upon entering) is believed to ensure pregnancy to any woman who steps over it, as a former Empress originally who was originally thought to be barren got pregnant after stepping over this stone. Along with a plethora of folk beliefs, the shrine is also a popular place to view flowers in the summertime. The shrine grounds are free, but to enter the shrine costs ¥500.

<u>Suzumushi-dera</u>. "Suzumushi-dera" means "cricket temple", and as you might guess, there is a large case of crickets all along the wall inside the temple. Ever since the temple was featured on the NHK, Japan's national television station, it has received quite large crowds of people waiting to enter, but don't let the crowds scare you away. The purpose is to enjoy the crickets chirping, so upon entering, visitors are treated to tea, a snack, and a speech by one of the temple's priests (in Japanese, of course) lasting roughly 20 minutes. He talks about the crickets and makes a shameless plug for the charms sold at the temple and then the next group is allowed in. The temple seats a large amount of people, so even those waiting on the steps should be able to get in for the next session. In

order to keep the crickets chirping, they have to keep the temple warm, making it great for winter travellers.

<u>Kokedera</u>, 56 Jingatani-cho, Matsuo. 075-391-3631. The temple will tell you when your reservation is scheduled for in their response letter if you have been accepted. Kokedera, also known as Saiho-ji, is one of Kyoto's World Heritage Sites famous for is beautiful moss garden. In the past, visitors could come and go freely, like most temples however, due to tourists stepping on and killing the moss, the temple had to limit the number of visitors and now requires a reservation in order to visit. The only accepted method is by postal mail at least one week in advance, preferably at least three. You need to send a letter giving them your name, the number of people in your party, and the date(s) you prefer to visit along with a self-addressed stamped envelope for them to send their response back to you. If already in Japan you can request an "ofuku hagaki" and if outside of Japan you can request an International Reply Coupon (IRC) to

cover the postage. Here is the temple's address: Saiho-ji Temple 56 Jingatani-cho, Matsuo Nishikyo-ku, Kyoto, 615-8286, Japan

You are unable to choose the hour of the visit, and if very busy on your requested day they may suggest a day earlier or later, so it will help to be flexible in your schedule. You must be punctual or else you may be denied entry. Be aware also that photos of Kokedera on images.google.com or elsewhere are mostly from the garden at its height of beauty, which is in summer or autumn. If visiting in winter or through the first half of spring, you are likely to find the moss yellowed out or barren. The garden looks far better from June (but the unrelenting rain of the rainy season may dampen your experience) though autumn's changing colors. Some may still find the visit worth it overall. If accepted, you will pay on arrival. While the price is quite steep, keep in mind that along with a tour of the garden, you will also listen to a monk recite sutras and even get to copy the sutras yourself. You will need to sit on your legs or crosslegged for nearly an hour. If that is not possible you may be able to request a low chair to use. For those lucky enough to be accepted for a visit, it is often one of their best memories. Admission is ¥3000 (the most expensive temple in Kyoto)

Doing

Hozu River Cruise, (For a 16km trip down the river take the JR Sagano Line from JR Kyoto station to JR Kameoka Station (approx. 20 minutes by rapid express) and turn left when you exit the station. It is a 10 minute walk to the boarding site along a rather busy road.). Departures run from mid March to the end of November roughly on the hour starting at 9 AM. Last boat leaves at 3:30pm. During the winter boats with heated seats leave at 10am,11:30am, 1pm and 2:30pm.. To experience Arashiyama to the fullest, the river cruise is your best bet! A variety of boats, small or large, both rowed and motored, are waiting on either side of the river. Be sure to confirm how far and for how long the trip goes, though. Some are as long as two hours, and others will do a quick turnaround in less then twenty minutes. Be prepared to get splashed and take appropriate precautions for electronic equipment. The drop off point sets you down just outside the entrance to Iwatayama Monkey Park, a great location to begin your stroll around the sights of Arashiyama. It costs ¥ 3,900 for adults, ¥ 2,500 for children.

Ride in a Rickshaw, 075-864-4444. For those looking to experience Kyoto from a different perspective, travelling in a rickshaw allows you to do just that. You can arrange where they will take you (and check the fees, of course) and then they will take a picture of you inside the rickshaw. Depending on where you are, you may even be able to get the Togetsukyo Bridge in the background. While you travel, the rickshaw puller will tell you about the area and the local sites, so you can learn a lot, if you understand Japanese. You can find the rickshaws around Togetsukyo Bridge. Prices range from about ¥5000-7000, depending on where you go

<u>Sagano Romantic Train</u>. Trains depart from Torokko Saga Station every hour from 8:50 AM to 4:50 PM and from Torokko Arashiyama Station every hour from 8:53 AM to 4:53 PM. A scenic ride on a steam train through the Arashiyama area taking you as far as Kameoka. Many people enjoy riding the train to Kameoka and then taking the Hozu River Cruise back to Arashiyama. ¥600.

<u>Fufunoyu Hot Springs</u>, (*north of Hankyu-Arashiyama station, near the river*). 12pm-10pm. A modest but clean and modern hot spring complex, with both indoor and outdoor baths for each sex. A great way to relax after a long day in Arashiyama and sample the onsen experience, without trekking to a mountain resort or an expensive ryokan stay. Just make sure you brush up on your etiquette first! Adults from ¥1300 (including towel hire).

Buying

Most of the areas shops and dining are located along Tenryuji Tsukurimichi-cho, which runs from the Togetsukyo Bridge up to Seiryoji Temple.

<u>JJ Sagano</u>, 40-1 Tsukurimichi-cho, +81 075 882-0775. 10AM-6PM. Closed Tues. A nice souvenir shop with a variety of Hello Kitty goods, as well as many local souvenirs.

Eating

<u>Cafe Rue Ribera</u>, (*Near Enmachi Station on the Sagano Line.*), +81 075 812-2351. W-M 11:30AM-2:30PM. A small restaurant and bar. The owner speaks English.

<u>Aka Manma</u>, 26 Setogawa-cho, Saga Tenryuji, Ukyo-ku (*North of Togetsukyō Bridge, near the JR line.*), +81 075 881-9073 (fax: +81 075 861-0285). 10AM-11PM, lunch 11:30AM-3PM, dinner 5PM-9PM. Café and restaurant. Serves a mix of French, Italian, and Japanese dishes. English menu and vegetarian options available.

Shinpachi Tea House, 20-40 Saga Tenryuji Tsukurimichi-cho, +81 075 861-0117. 9AM-6PM. Despite being called a teahouse, Shinpachi is popular for its gelatto ice cream. They also have ice cream cones and parfaits. It is also a souvenir shop, so visitors often enjoy eating their gelatto while browsing the shop. Gelatto single ¥350, double ¥400.

Shintogetsu +81 075 882-9884. 11AM-5PM. Serves a variety of meal set, with soba and the famous Yodofu (tofu) being among the most popular.

Hirokawa, 48-1 Saga Tenryuji Kitatsukurimichi-cho, +81 075 871-5226. Tu-Su 11:30AM-2:30PM, 5PM-10PM. A great restaurant for those who enjoy eating eel. ¥1575-¥4200.

Mellow Cafe, Arashiyamakamikawaracho,1-3, Kyoto Nishikyo-ku (FROM San-in Line Kyoto Station By local train to San-in Line Sagaarashiyama Station (20minutes) from San-in Line Sagaarashiyama Station by walk (15minutes)), 075-864-2020.

《TUES~FRI・SUN》 11:00～18:00（L.O.17:30）

《SAT》 11:00～19:00(L.O.18:30) Monday Closed. Mellow Cafe is right by the Togetsukyo River. The terrace has a beautiful view of Arashiyama. Enjoy the popular Kyoto original hot-dogs (Kyoto-dogs). 1000 yen ~ 2000yen.

ExCafe, 35-3 Sagatenryuji Tsukurimichicho Ukyo-ku Kyoto Kyoto (*73 meters from Arashiyama.*) 075-882-6366. 10:00～17:30. It is well known as an old Japanese-style house cafe, that has traditional Japanese sweets such as, odango, zenzai, and maccha parfait, and you can relax with it by the soothing atmosphere. Most popular menu is the odango, which you can roast it yourself. Odango comes with a mini-size Japanese small charcoal grill. ¥1,000~¥1,999.

Sleeping

Most travelers will stay in Central or Northern Kyoto instead, and visit Arashiyama only for the day.

Business Hotel Arashiyama, Arashiyamakamikawaracho,1-3, Kyoto Nishikyo-ku (FROM San-in Line Kyoto Station By local train to San-in Line Sagaarashiyama Station (20minutes) from San-in Line Sagaarashiyama Station by walk (15minutes)),

Budget

Temple lodgings

Rokuō-in, 24 Kitahori-cho, Saga, Ukyo-ku (*Near Arashimaya, six minutes by foot from Saga-Arashiyama Station on the JR Sagano Line*),+81 (0)75-861-1645. Only for female visitors. 10 rooms with a maximum capacity of 30; during peak season, guests traveling alone may be asked to share a room with another single guest; towels not provided; one bath. Crowded during autumn foliage season. Curfew at 7:30pm. Closed during New Year's holidays. ¥4,500 per person with breakfast.

Hostels

Bola Bola Guest House, 25-17 Horigauchi-cho Uzumasa, Ukyo-ku (*near JR Uzumasa train station on the western part of Kyoto, 15 min. train ride from Kyoto station*), +81 (0)75-861-5663. checkin: 3 PM - midnight; checkout: 11 AM. A friendly and well kept guest house. The owner speaks English and is very willing to help foreign guests. ¥2500 dorm, ¥3500 private room (¥2500 each for 2 or more people).

<u>Utano Youth Hostel</u>, 9 Nakayama-cho, Uzumasa, 075-462-2288. checkin: 3:00 to 11:30 PM; checkout: 10:00 AM. A convenient and affordable hostel in Arashiyama. They offer bike rentals for ¥600/day (or ¥200/hour), allowing you to easily see most of Arashiyama or explore much of Northwestern Kyoto in a day. They also have their own tennis court and barbeque grill available for use by guests. Reservations can be made online. Prices start at ¥3300 (¥2800 for ages 18 and under)

Higashiyama

Some of the most picturesque parts of Kyoto are located in the eastern region of the city, across the

Kamo River. Visiting the main tourist attractions of eastern Kyoto will fill a full day - a suggested itinerary is to work north from Kiyomizu-dera to Ginkakuji, passing through Gion, and visiting Yasaka Shrine and Nanzenji before following the Philosopher's Walk to Ginkakuji.

Getting in

By train

Keihan Railway serves the entire area of Eastern Kyoto, offering easy access to every part of the area. It also connects the Eastern region to Northern Kyoto at Demachiyanagi Station, from which Shimogamo Shrine is in walking distance, or cross the street to Eizan Railway Demachiyanagi Station to go as far as Kurama. Keihan Railway travels south to Southern Kyoto, extending as far away as Hirakata and Osaka, and offering easy connections to Uji at Chushojima Station.

By subway

Travellers staying in Central Kyoto can easily reach the Higashiyama area using the municipal subway system's Tōzai Line. For tourists, the most convenient stops on this line are probably Higashiyama Station (north of Gion) and Keage Station (near Nanzen-ji). The subway is also convenient for those travelling onward to Otsu and Lake Biwa.

By bus
Numerous Kyoto City Bus routes traverse the neighborhood, particularly along the major north-south thoroughfare, Higashioji-dori. Route 100 is the most convenient for tourists: it runs from Kyoto Station to Ginkakuji, stopping only at major attractions. Useful local routes include #5, Kyoto Station Shijo-Karasuma Gion Ginkakuji, and #206, Kyoto Station Sanjusangendo Gion Chionji Kitaoji (in northern Kyoto).

Seeing
Kiyomizu Temple, 1-chome, Kiyomizu, Higashiyama-ku (*Nearest bus stop: Kiyomizu-michi, routes 100, 202, 206, 207*), 075-551-123. Daily: 6-18. This temple complex, with a spectacular location overlooking the city, is a deservedly popular attraction, approached by either of two tourist-filled souvenir-shop-lined streets,

Kiyomizu-zaka or Chawan-zaka. Admission ¥300. Open daily, 6am-6pm. *Nearest bus stop: Kiyomizu-michi or Gojo-zaka*. *Highlights of the temple* complex include; The main hall's wooden veranda, supported by hundreds of pillars and offering incredible views over the city.

Jishu Shrine, the love-themed shrine selling countless charms to help you snag the one you love, and featuring two "love stones" positioned around 18m apart which the lovelorn must walk between with their eyes closed to confirm their loved one's affection, and Otowa-no-taki the temple's waterfall, which gives it its name (Kiyomizu literally means 'pure water'). Visitors stand beneath the waterfall, and collect water to drink by holding out little tin cups. Mountain hike, if you're up for a mountain walk, steer to the right-hand pathway instead of taking the left toward the Jishu-jinja. The path leads through a gate and winds up onto the mountain. You can walk up for a good hour and not reach the end of the path. Has lovely forest and great scenery, and makes for a nice short excursion out of the city traffic. ¥300.

<u>Mount Daimonji</u>. Mount Daimonji is a bit more than a hill, but it provides a breathtaking (and perhaps the best) view of the city. So if you're in the mood for a hike, this is a pleasant forest walk, taking about an hour. At the summit, you can take a breather and check out the views over the city, or climb the steps and keep hiking through the forest at the top for hours, as long as you don't mind winding up far away from where you started. There's a clearly marked path up the mountain that begins near Ginkakuji. To reach the trailhead, turn left when facing the gates of Ginkakuji, and, before the stone torii (the iconic gate found throughout Japan), turn right and follow the path upwards. You'll soon be greeted with a map of the hill. If you don't know Japanese, don't worry, just follow everyone up the very-obvious path to the summit.

<u>Rokuharamitsu-ji</u>, 81-1 Rokuro-cho 2-chome, Matsubara-dori, Higashiyama-ku, 075-561-6980. Daily

8-17. While the temple itself may not seem so special, the trip is made worthwhile by the amazing Kamakura Period artwork housed in its museum. In particular, the statue of Kuya is quite a unique piece of artwork depicting Kuya Shonin reciting the nenbutsu. To depict the words, the artist Taira Kiyomori, sculpted six miniature figures of Kuya Shonin walking out of his open mouth. Each figure represents one syllable in the nenbutsu. This temple is also the 17th temple of the Saigoku Kannon Pilgrimage. Grounds: free, Museum: ¥500.

Sanjusangen-do, "Sanjūsangendō (*Nearest bus stop: Hakubutsukan Sanjusangendo-mae, routes 100, 206, 208*), 075-561-0467. Open from 8 AM to 5 PM. is definitely worth a visit. It was founded in 1164 and became famous for its 1001 beautiful wooden and gold-leaf covered statues of Kannon, goddess of mercy, housed in thirty-three bays (sanjusan = thirty-three, gendo = bays) in the main hall. Entrance fee: ¥600.

<u>Kyoto National Museum</u>, 527 Chayamachi, Higashiyama-ku, 075-541-1151. 9:30am - 5:00pm, closed Mondays. Is near Sanjusangen-do, and has a large collection of ancient Japanese sculpture, ceramics, metalwork, painting, and other artifacts. (It's quite similar to the Tokyo National Museum in Tokyo/Ueno.) The Museum building is fairly grand, but the statue of Rodin's *The Thinker* out front is a bit out of place, as there's no Western art inside. It's seven minutes east of Shichijo Keihan. admission ¥500.

<u>Yogen-in</u>. The original temple was built by one of Hideyoshi Toyotomi's concubines in honor of her father, but the temple was destroyed by a fire. When rebuilding the temple, the floorboards of Fushimi Castle in Southern Kyoto were used to construct the ceiling. Since Fushimi Castle was the site of quite a bloody battle, when you look at the ceiling, you can still see blood stains and body outlines from soldiers who committed seppuku.

The artwork in the temple is also very famous, particularly the elephant paintings. Non-Japanese visitors have mixed success trying to enter the temple. You may be shown an English write-up that states that only those who understand Japanese are able to enter (because everyone who enters will be greeted by a guide who will walk you through the temple). It ends with something like, "This is why you are not allowed to enter the temple." Alternatively, the staff may refuse you entry and ask you to leave. Try not to let this deter you if you really want to enter but don't know Japanese. Simply agree to the tour, pay the fee, maybe lie about your Japanese ability, and then politely pay attention to your guide as they walk you through the temple.

Okazaki area

Heian Shrine, 97 Nishi Tennocho, Okazaki, Sakyo-ku, 075-761-0221. Mar-Aug:8:30-17:30; Sep-Oct: 8:30-17; Nov-Feb: 8:30-16. Built in 1895 in commemoration of the 1100th anniversary of Kyoto, the shrine was designed as a scaled-down replica of the original Imperial Palace. The Shin'en Garden encircling the backside of the shrine is one of the city's most beautiful gardens and a popular place for *hanami*, particularly for those who prefer pink blossoms. Grounds: free; Garden: ¥600.

<u>Kyoto Municipal Museum of Art</u>, Okazaki Park, Sakyo-ku, 075-771-4107,. Open 9 AM to 5 PM. Closed Mondays. This museum houses a wide variety of art with the permanent collections featuring artists that are from Kyoto. Special exhibits may feature Japanese art from other areas or foreign artwork.

<u>Kyoto National Museum of Modern Art</u>, Okazaki Enshoji-cho, Sakyo-ku, 075-761-4111. 9:30 AM to 5:00 PM (on Fridays during special exhibitions, hours may be extended to 8:00 PM). Closed Mondays. An interesting museum featuring works from famous, as well as up-and-coming modern artists. Exhibits change frequently, so its best to call or visit the webisite to see exactly what will featured during your visit. You may

also want to make sure they will not be changing exhibitions, as they often close an entire floor of the museum during the transition.¥420. (college students receive a discount and special exhibitions require additional costs).

Yoshida Shrine, 30 Kaguraoka-cho, Yoshida, Sakyo-ku, 075-771-3788. All day. Most famous as the site of the Setsubun Festival held in February, this small shrine was very highly revered during the Heian Period, and the court made offerings here. Free.

Kyoto City Zoo, Okazaki Houshoji-cho, Sakyo-ku (*located on the east side of the Kyoto Municipal Art Museum*), 075-771-0210. Like most zoos, visitors will see lions, tigers, and monkeys. There is an aviary and reptile exhibit, as well. The zoo has some native Japanese animals, but there isn't much to set it apart from most other zoos in the world.

Hosomi Art Museum, 6-3 Okazaki, Saishoji-cho, 075-752-5555. Open from 10 AM to 6 PM. Closed Mon. A museum that showcases Japanese religious art from all periods of history. Exhibits change each season but typically feature famous artwork from local temples and shrines. Prices vary depending on the exhibit.

Maruyama Park area

Maruyama Park, 625 Gion-machi, Kitagawa-ku. is the main center for cherry blossom viewing in Kyoto, and can get extremely crowded at that time of year. The park's star attraction is a weeping cherry tree (*shidarezakura*). Main entrance to the park is through Yasaka Shrine. Admission is free.

Kodaiji Temple, 526, Shimogawara-cho, Kodai-ji, Higashiyama-ku, 075-561-9966,. Open from 9 AM to 5 PM. This temple was built for Toyotomi Hideyoshi's widow by Tokugawa Ieyasu and is located right next to the Ryozen Kannon temple. If you really like temples this is a very nice one. It's got a nice bamboo grove that you walk through on the way out. If you're in the area it's a good sight to see. Entrance fee: ¥600.

Chion-in. 075-531-2111. The head temple of the Jodo sect of Buddhism. The Sanmon gate at the entrance to the temple is the largest of such gates in the nation. Visitors can walk freely around the complex and inside the buildings, except for those that house the temples "Seven Wonders". Walking the temple grounds is free, but seeing the wonders costs money.

Shoren-in, 69-1 Sanjobo-cho, 075-561-2345. Open from 9 AM to 5 PM. Once associated with the head Tendai Buddhist sect temple, Enryaku-ji on Mount Hiei, Shoren-in is considered to be one of the top five Tendai sect temples. During the Tokugawa period, it served as temporary lodging for a retired emperor after the Imperial Palace burned down. Those who come during November may be able to practice a tea ceremony (See "Do" section of the guide). Admission is ¥500.

Higashi Otani Mausoleum. Located in a cemetary, tourists typically visit this site accidentally however, because some of the ashes of Shinran, the founder of Jodo-Shin Buddhism, are contained inside the mausoleum, it is a popular place for Buddhists to come to pay their respects. Entrance to the grounds is free.

<u>Ryozen Kannon Statue</u>, Kodaiji Shimokawaracho, Higashiyama-ku (*At the northern end of Ninen-zaka*), 075 561 2205. Daily 8:30-16:30. A memorial to the unknown Japanese soldiers who died in World War II, with a 24-meter-tall statue of Kannon. Admission is ¥200, including a lit incense stick to place in front of the temple.

<u>Ryozen History Museum</u>, 1 Ryozen-cho Seikanji. Open from 10 AM to 4 PM. Closed Mondays. A museum dedicated to displaying artifacts and information about the Meiji Period.

<u>Ryozen Gokoku Shrine</u>, 605 Seikan-ji-Ryosen-cho, 075-561-7124. This shrine was built to house the souls of all those who died in the Pacific War, from the Meiji Restoration uprisings and the Russo-Japanese War to the end of World War II. It is the first shrine in the

nation to be officially recognized as a shrine for war dead.

Gion district

The flagstone-paved streets and traditional buildings of the Gion district, located to the north-west of Kiyomizu-dera, are where you're most likely to see geishas in Kyoto, scurrying between buildings or slipping into a taxi. The area just to the north of Shijo-dori, to the west of Yasaka Shrine, is especially photogenic - particularly around Shinbashi-dori and Hanami-koji. Sannen-zaka ("three-year-slope") and Ninen-zaka ("two-year-slope"), two stepped streets leading off from Kiyomizu-zaka, are also very picturesque - but watch your step, slipping over on these streets brings three or two years' bad luck respectively.

Yasaka Shrine, 625 Gion-machi, Kitagawa-ku (*East end of Shijo-dori. Nearest bus stop: Gion*), 075-561-6155. Always open. At the eastern end of Shijo-dori, at the edge of Gion, is the shrine responsible for Kyoto's main festival - the Gion Matsuri, which takes place in July. The shrine is small in comparison with many in Kyoto, but it boasts an impressive display of lanterns. Admission is free.

<u>Kenninji Temple</u>, 584 Komatsu-cho, Higashiyama-ku, 075-561-0190. 10:00-16:00 daily. Japan's oldest Zen temple, has handsome halls and sand and moss gardens, and is of particular interest to art lovers. Sotatsu's famed Edo-period screens of the Wind and Thunder Gods are on display. And on the high ceiling of the Hatto Dharma Hall writhe Koizumi Junsaku's splendid Twin Dragons, painted and installed in 2002. Admission is ¥500.

Philosopher's Path
The Philosopher's Path runs from Ginkakuji down to Eikando, with many travellers choosing to end their journey at Nanzenji (or begin, should you choose to walk towards Ginkakuji). The sites are listed in the order you will pass them if you start from Ginkakuji.

Ginkakuji, Ginkakuji-cho (*Nearest bus stop: Ginkakuji-michi, routes 5, 17, 32, 100, 102, 203, 204*), 075-771-5725. Mar-Nov: 08:30-17:00; Dec-Mar: 09:00-16:30. This temple, known as the Silver Pavilion, is at the northern end of the Philosopher's Walk. Much like its golden counterpart Kinkakuji, the Silver Pavilion is often choked with tourists, shuffling past a scrupulously-maintained dry landscape Zen garden and the surrounding moss garden, before posing for pictures in front of the Pavilion across a pond. Do note, however, that major restoration works are being done on the pavilion, which is now surrounded by metal scaffolding. This is not expected to be completed until after 2010. *Unlike* its counterpart, however, the Silver Pavilion was never actually covered in silver; only the name had been applied before the plans fell apart. Be sure not to miss the display of *Very Important Mosses*! Admission ¥500.

Honen-in 075-771-2420. Open from 7 AM to 4 PM. A quiet temple with some interesting raised sand designs. It was built in honor of Honen, the founder of the Jodo sect. Temple grounds are free.

Anraku-ji, 21 Shishigatani, 075-771-5360. A temple built to console the soles of Anraku and some concubines who were killed by order of the Imperial Court who did not approve of their Buddhist sect.

Koun-ji, 075-751-7949. A temple designed around the borrowed scenery of the surrounding mountains, it was once owned by Empress Gomizuno.

Nyakuoji Shrine, 2 Nishioji Sakyo-ku, 075-771-7420. A nice shrine to visit in the autumn when the leaves are changing. It's a worthwhile stop for those travelling along the Philosopher's Path, but probably not worth making the trip just to see this shrine. Entrance is free.

Eikando Temple , 48 Eikando-cho, Sakyo-ku (*Nearest bus stop: Nanzenji/Eikando-michi, route 5*), 075-761-0007. Daily 9-17. A large temple said to have been originally constructed by Priest Kukai. The temple features a unique statue of Amida Buddha, Mikaeri

Amida, that looks to the right rather than facing forward. The temple grounds also feature a Tahoto pagoda and a lake. The temple is particularly pleasant in the autumn when the leaves are changing. ¥600.

<u>Nanzenji Temple</u>, Fukuchi-cho, Nanzenji, Sakyo-ku (*Nearest bus stop: Nanzenji/Eikando-michi, route 5*). 8:40a.m.-5:00p.m.(until 4:30p.m. from Dec to Feb). with its distinctive two-story entrance gate (*sanmon*) and aqueduct, is another popular temple in Kyoto, but its larger size means that it doesn't seem as crowded as many of the others. Nearest bus stop: Nanzenji, Eikando-michi. Nearest subway station: Keage. Open daily, 8.30am-5pm. Walking around the temple complex is free, including the unusual Meiji-era aqueduct that wouldn't look out of place in Italy. There are three regions of Nanzenji that you can pay to enter: Sanmon - the two-story main gate to Nanzenji Temple charges ¥500 for admission, and offers pleasant views over the surrounding area of the city. Nanzen-in Zen Temple - a small, but relaxing temple and moss garden

behind the aqueduct, dating back to the 13th century, charges ¥300 for admission, and is probably only worth it if you have a particular interest in Zen Buddhism. Hojo - the abbot's quarters, is a more interesting building, with a small raked gravel garden and some impressive paintings on the sliding doors of the buildings. Admission is ¥500.

Doing

During warmer months, Japanese and foreigners alike gather on the banks of the Kamo River to drink and make merry. The area around the Sanjo Bridge is the most popular. It's a friendly, welcoming scene. In summer months, on Fridays and Saturdays, a group of fire dancers and drum players occasionally hold free performances.

Walk the Philosopher's Path. The 2km-long path through north-eastern Kyoto, along which a philosophy professor, Kitaro Nishida, used to frequently walk. It is a surprisingly pleasant and relaxing walk even today, though you will undoubtedly share it with more tourists than Kitaro did. The walk runs south from Ginkakuji beside an aqueduct to Nyakuoji Shrine, many guidebooks suggest that the walk continues further south from there to Nanzenji, but this southerly section of the walk is less consistently signposted. The route passes several temples *en route*, notably Honen-in, a beautiful secluded temple with a thatched gate. The best time to walk the trail is in the spring when the cherry blossoms are in bloom, as the path is lined with cherry trees, or in the fall when the leaves are changing. Of course, these are also the most crowded times of year.

<u>Ride in a Rickshaw</u>, 075-533-0444. Unlike the days of old when rickshaw pullers were looked down upon, the men pulling them today are quite highly regarded (and highly attractive). Some of the most popular pullers may even have their own patrons. These men do not simply transport you; they also act as guides, sharing information about the area and attractions. For those

who can understand Japanese, it can be as informative as it is fun. The rickshaws are particularly popular with couples, as it can be quite romantic, especially in the evenings. The drivers are very friendly and will gladly take a picture of you sitting in it to remember the experience. Although they do have some set routes, you can also request to be taken to a specific attraction (within a reasonable distance, of course). Rickshaws can be found throughout the area from outside Maruyama Park to Kiyomizu-dera. Prices vary depending on what route you choose, but they typically range from ¥5000-7000.

Tea Ceremony at Shoren-in. Open from 10 AM to 3:30 PM on the vernal equinox, May 5, and throughout November. The ceremony is held in the former study of retired Emperor Gosakuramachi known as the Kobun-tei, typically not open to visitors. The room was rebuilt in the 1990s after a fire burned down the original, but it is still an interesting place nonetheless, and the tea ceremony is an interesting experience. The ceremony costs ¥1000 in addition to the temple entrance fee, costing ¥1500 total.

Riraku Spa, Hyatt Regency Kyoto Hotel, 644-2 Sanjusangendo-mawari, Higashiyama-ku, 075-541-1234. Seemingly expensive. I would advise going to Takayama for a luxurious yet affordable spa experience (¥10,000)

Geisha and Maiko

Geisha Walking Lecture If your are interested about the world of the Geisha, you shouldn't miss the walking lecture by Peter MacIntosh . The walk will have you tour the Gion district where Peter, will give you an insider's view into the past, present and future of this unique and exotic world. If you're lucky you might see a Geisha walking by to one of her appointments. Reservation is to be made by phone: +81 090-5169-1654

Kyoto Cuisine and Maiko Evening, 505 Gion-machi minami-gawa, Higashiyama-ku, 075-541-5315. Show lasts from 6 PM to 10 PM Events held on Mon., Wed., Fri., Sat., and other chosen days. Located at Gion Hatanaka, this event offers foreigners the rare opportunity to see an authentic performance by real maiko. Guests are served food and you can drink as much as you like during the performance. You can make reservations online (continue to check for updates, because they reserve the right to cancel performances).¥18000 (includes all-you-can-drink).

<u>Photo session as Maiko/Geiko</u>, 4F Ouka Bldg., 576 Gion-cho Minamigawa Shijo-tori Hanamikoji Nishi-iru Higashiyama-ku (*Gion*), 075-661-0858. 10:00am - 8:00pm. If you are interested in having a photo session dressed up as a Maiko or Geiko (geisha) or, for men, as a samurai, several studios in Kyoto provide this service at affordable price. The session includes full make up and dress in a kimono and normally lasts for 1.5-2 hours. Options include indoor or outdoor shots (strolling in Gion dressed up as a geisha!), plus at Yumekoubou they will take a few photos with your

own camera while they dress you up, for free. It is recommended to select a plan and make reservation online - in some studios they speak very limited English.

Buying

Rakushisha Paper Crafts, 549-2 Nishinomon-cho (*On Shijo-dori where it intersects with Yamato-Oji-dori near Sanjuusangendo*), 075-561-5852. Open from 10 AM to 5:30 PM. A great souvenir shop with some more original and less tacky souvenirs. In particular, for those looking to purchase nice nice paintings or copies of famous Japanese paintings, this shop offers a variety of paintings on paper that looks less cheesy than those that you will find along Shijo or near Kiyomizu-dera. There are also authentic Kyoto-made paper fans. Much of the items in this store are difficult to find elsewhere, so if you're interested in these items, it's best to buy them here.

Honkenishio Yatsuhashi, 075-541-8284. Open from 8 AM to 6 PM. The best store to buy raw yatsuhashi, it offers the largest variety of flavors, including seasonal varieties. One package of yatsuhashi costs ¥250.

Eating

Il Pappalardo, 075-533-3330. Lunch from 11:30 AM to 3:00 PM, Dinner from 5:30 PM to 10:00 PM. One of Kyoto's best Italian restaurants. Dishes tend to be pricey, but the food tastes delicious. Pizzas are sold at more affordable prices. Pizzas range from ¥1500-2400.

Kick-up Bar is outside the Keage Tozai line subway station (nearest Exit 1) and on the opposite side of the street from the Westin Miyako Hotel. They have the best meatball sandwich in Japan and loaded pizza made from homemade dough. The food is good, and the owner and his son are American and speak English. A nonsmoking establishment.

Santouka Ramen is a Hokkaido style ramen shop in the Sanjo-Keihan above-ground plaza & bus station. For about ¥900 they have excellent pork broth ramen. Don't forget the broth-boiled egg for ¥200. Look for the line outside.

<u>Saryou Tsuriji</u>, 075-561-2257. Open from 10 AM to 9 PM. Famous for its macha (grean tea) parfait, this restaurant is quite popular among Japanese tourists. It is not uncommon to wait 30 minutes just to get inside. Mainly ice cream is served, and most of it is grean tea flavored, as it is a Kyoto specialty. It's a nice experience for those who like to make eating part of their travel experience, but for those on a budget, there are plenty of vendors selling cheap macha ice cream cones. Dishes typically range from ¥1000-1400.

<u>Sweets Paradise</u>, Koto Cross Hankyu Kawaramachi 6th Floor, 075-212-2234. Open from 10:30 AM to 9:30 PM. Sweets Paradise is the famed all-you-can-eat cake and dessert restaurant. While they do offer some main dishes, no one comes here for anything but the sweets! After you pay, you can eat as much as you want for 90 minutes. ¥1480.

TACkitchen (Tac Kitchen Gion Store), Yusaka-machi Yasaka Shinchi, Higashiyama Ward, Kyoto City 8 8 – 1 (Coming from Gion Shijo station, walk along Shijo Dori on the left side, towards the east. After the first crossroads with traffic lights, walk about 100 meters and turn left into the small street. About 50 meters after the next crossroads, TACkitchen is on your left. Ground floor, wooden sliding door.), 075-531-0970,. 6-3pm. Not the cheapest, but really great Italian food in a very hospitable environment, with friendly staff, nice music and great dessert. 4000 p.p.

Torikizoku (Bird aristocrat). 5 or 6 pm to late. Torikizoku is the most popular yakitori chain in Kansai. There are several locations in Kyoto - most convenient for travellers is in Kawaramachi/Shijo, just before the bridge, or between sanjo and shijo, on kiyachou-dori. The yakitori is delicious, comes in generous serves and is very cheap. It's very popular with both locals and expats, and is always busy. Try to come before 7:30 to secure seats. Look for the Japanese characters on the distinctive yellow and red sign. All food/drink ¥300 each.

Vietnam Frog Located just above Sanjo-Keihan station this nice little Vietnamese place as pho and other favorites at a moderate price: approx. ¥800-1500.

Drinking

New Supper (New Supper " nyuusapaa "), 53 Okazaki Tennou-cho, 075-771-3019. Open from 6 PM to 2 AM. Closed Mondays. ¥600 for whiskey and brandy, ¥800 for a cocktail fizz.

Pig & Whistle: underwent a renovation last year, adding a more stylish whiskey bar to its original drinks bar. This is a popular spot, located right above the Sanjo Keihan subway station. If you hear live music, go on up; though it probably won't be great music, it will draw a crowd. Food here is also mediocre.

The Gael Irish Pub: (formerly known as "Tadg's Irish Pub") convenient location if you are downtown (located in Gion at Shijo and Kawabata-dori). Open mic nights can be a mixed bag depending on who comes (always excellent jazz, no longer holding poetry readings apparently). Great portions of food. Definitely go for rugby games.

Kickup. Kick-up Bar is outside the Keage Tozai line subway station (nearest Exit 1) and on the opposite side of the street from the Westin Miyako Hotel. They have the best meatball sandwich in Japan and loaded pizza made from homemade dough. The food is good, and the owner and his son are American and speak English. A nonsmoking establishment.

Sleeping

The small size and historic preservation of this district leave little room for hotels most people will stay in Central Kyoto instead. There are a few exceptions:

Budget

Hostels

bAKpAK Kyoto Hostel, 1-234 Miyagawa Suji, Higashiyama-ku (*between Kawaramachi and Gion, next* to the Minamiza theater), +81 (0)75-525-3143. Dorm ¥2500/person to Japanese-style quad ¥14,000/room.

Gojo Guest House, 3-396-2 Gojobashi-higashi, Higashiyama-Ku (*5 min. walk from Keihan Gojo Station*), +81 075-525-2299. checkin: 3-10 PM; checkout: 11 AM. A Japanese style hostel with a cozy cafe located in the Higashiyama area. Dorm ¥2500/person, twin ¥6000/room, triple ¥9900/room for three people, ¥12,000 for four.

Guest House - The Earth Ship, 33-15 Naka-Adaticho, Yoshida, Sakyo-ku (*near Kyoto University, 10 min. walk from Keihan Demachiyanagi Station*), +81 (0)75-204-0077. Friendly shared living room. Dormitory ¥2,500, Private room starts at ¥4000 for one person, ¥6000 for two people, ¥7500 for three, ¥8000 for four. There is an additional discount on these prices for long stays.

Higashiyama Youth Hostel, 112 Goken-machi Shirakawabashi (*Located just across the bridge from Higashiyama Station on the Subway Tozai Line*), 075-

761-8135. checkin: 3:30-7:30 PM; checkout: 9:00 AM. A hotel conveniently located between sites around Maruyama Park and the Okazaki area. There is a 10:00 PM. Reservations can be made at the site. Costs ¥3960 per night without meals, ¥3360 for members.

Midrange
<u>Hidden Inn Kyoto Vacation Rental Townhouse</u>, Kyoto-shi Higashiyama-ku Kamitoryo-cho 126-12 (*5 min. walk southeast from Keihan Gojo station*), +81 (0)50-5534-2429. checkin: 4 PM; checkout: 10 AM. Modern & luxurious centrally located vacation rental townhouse fully equipped with kitchen, 2 bedrooms with Western style beds (sleeps up to 6), free WIFI. A great option for families or small groups. from ¥19,500 for two.

<u>Kyoto Travelers Inn</u>, 91 Enshojicho, Okazaki, Sakyoku (*7 min. walk northeast from Higashiyama subway station T10, exit 1, or get off at Heian-jingu-torii-mae stop on number 5 bus*) +81 (0)75-771-0225 (fax: +81 (0)75-771-0226). checkin: 3 PM; checkout: 10 AM. One of the few hotels in eastern Kyoto, near the giant concrete *torii* of

the Heian-jingu shrine. The building is divided into two sections, with Japanese-style and Western-style rooms; the former are often booked solid by groups during the school year, but are preferable if you're OK with a futon instead of actual bed. Free Wi-Fi in the lobby. Singles ¥6825 and up, doubles ¥12,600 and up.

Splurge
Iori Gion Shinmonzen Townhouse, Shinmonzen-dori. Located in a traditional *machiya*, the Gion Shinmonzen (one of the Iori Machiya) is perfect for anyone looking to enhance their experience in Kyoto with ultra-traditional accommodations right in Gion. Prices start at ¥35000 (2 people) but vary depending on the day and time of year.

Hyatt Regency Kyoto, 644-2 Sanjusangendo-mawari, Higashiyama-ku (*Near Shichi-jo station on the Keihan line, or you can take buses #206, #208, or #100 from JR Kyoto station*) +81 075-541-1234. 5 star hotel with contemporary interior design. All its restaurants feature show kitchens, which is a first in Kyoto. ¥43,000 for twin room.

<u>Ryokan Tamahan</u>, 477 Gion, Shimogawara-cho, Higashiyama-ku (*Gion District, 10 minutes by taxi from Kyoto Station*), +81 075-561-3188. checkin: 3pm; checkout: 11am. Traditional Ryokan in quaint Gion district. It's worth the experience for at least one night. The price includes Japanese dinner and a choice of Japanese or Western breakfast. There is free wifi access. Staff are friendly but speak limited English. ¥25,000 per person.

<u>Westin Miyako Kyoto</u>, Keage, Sanjo, Higashiyama-ku, +81 (0)75-771-7111 (fax: +81 075-751-2490). checkin: 1 PM; checkout: 11AM. Established in 1890, this is the oldest Western-style hotel in Kyoto. It has over 400 rooms, starting at ¥33,000 for twins. (If you make a reservation through a travel agency, you may get a lower price.) It has about 30,000 square meters, and a few Japanese gardens, one of which, Aoiden was built by Jihei Ogawa. The gardens can be visited by non-

guests. It's near Keage Station (subway - Tozai Line, T09), or you can take a shuttle bus from JR Kyoto Station.

The KINOE, Higashioji Yasuikado higashiyama-ku Kyoto-city Japan 605 — 0812 +81-(0)75-561-1230 (fax: +81-75-561-8719). checkin: 3 PM; checkout: 11 AM. Traditional Japanese-style hotel situated at Gion district in Kyoto. It is located near Yasaka Shrine, Kodai-ji Temple, Kennin-ji Temple which is the first Zen Temple in Japan, Ninen-zaka, Sannen-zaka and Kiyomizu Temple.

Kyoto North.

Northern Kyoto is graced with scores of centuries-old shrines and temples, including several World Heritage Sites. One of Kyoto's most famous attractions - the magnificent golden pavilion of Kinkaku-ji - can be found here.

Getting in
By train

Keihan Railways connects North Kyoto with Eastern Kyoto at Demachiyanagi Station, the final stop on the line. On the Western side, Keifuku Railways provides easy access to the area from Arashiyama, with stops for Ninnaji, Ryoanji, Kinkakuji, and Kitano Tenmangu (Kitano Hakubaicho Station).

By subway
<u>Kitaōji Station</u> on the municipal subway system's Karasuma Line gives travellers easy access to a key bus terminal that serves parts of northern Kyoto. The Karasuma Line itself continues north all the way to Kokusaikaikan Station, near the Kyoto International Conference Center.

By bus
Northern Kyoto covers a large area, so many buses travel through the region. The #8 North (北8) bus makes a loop around the entire northern area. In the northwest, #59 passes most of the major attractions. In the northeast bus #4 and #5 each travel around popular touring spots.

The #8 is the only bus that will take you to and from the Takao area. The #17 bus will take you to the Ohara area. Both of these areas are located outside of the boundary of the ¥500 All-Day Bus pass, so do not purchase the pass if you are travelling to either of these areas.

Seeing

<u>North-western Kyoto</u>
Visiting the vast temple complexes of north-western Kyoto can take the better part of a day. A suggested itinerary is to take the subway (Karasuma line) to Kitaoji station, and walk west along Kitaoji-dori. Daitokuji, Kinkakuji, Ryoanji and Ninnaji Temples are all on Kitaoji-dori, and about 15-30 minutes' walk apart. However if it is summer time and sweltering hot it is easy to take the bus from temple to temple as well, just read the route map at the stops. En route, you will see the giant "dai" symbol burned on Mt. Daimon-ji, which can be climbed in an hour or so - look for the entrance near Ginkaku-ji (see below). If you're in Kyoto

at night on August 16th, look up - you'll see the aflame. Hirano Shrine is a short walk south along Nishioji-dori from Kinkakuji. If you still have time left at the end of the day, take the pleasant electric railway (Keifuku Kitano line) from Omuro to Katabiranotsuji, then take the JR Sagano line from nearby Uzumasa station back to central Kyoto.

<u>Kinkaku-ji Temple</u>, 1 Kinkakuji-cho, Kita-ku (*Nearest bus stops: Kinkakuji-michi (routes 12, 59, 101, 102, 204, 205) or Kinkakuji-mae (12 and 59)*), . Open daily 9 AM-5 PM. The Temple of the Golden Pavilion, formally known as Rokuonji , is the most popular tourist attraction in Kyoto. The pavilion was originally built as a retirement villa for Shogun Ashikaga Yoshimitsu in the late 14th century, and converted into a temple by his son. However, the pavilion was burnt down in 1950, by a young monk who had become obsessed with it. (The story became the basis for Yukio Mishima's novel *The Temple of the Golden Pavilion*.) The beautiful landscaping and the reflection of the temple on the

face of the water make for a striking sight, but keeping the mobs of visitors out of your photos will be a stern test for your framing abilities. Get there early if you can to beat the school groups. Visitors follow a path through the moss garden surrounding the pavilion, before emerging into a square crowded with gift shops. It's only a short walk from Ryōan-ji (below), making for an easy pairing (and study in contrasts). Admission fee is ¥400.

Ryōan-ji, (*Nearest bus stop: Ryōanji-mae, route 59; nearest Randen tram stop, Ryoanji-michi*), 075-463-2216, . Open daily 8 AM - 5 PM (Mar-Nov), 8:30 AM - 4:30 PM (Dec-Feb). Famous for its Zen garden, which is considered to be one of the most notable examples of the "dry-landscape" style. Surrounded by low walls, an austere arrangement of fifteen rocks sits on a bed of white gravel. That's it: no trees, no hills, no ponds, and no trickling water. Behind the simple temple that overlooks the rock garden is a stone washbasin called Tsukubai said to have been contributed by Tokugawa

Mitsukuni in the 17th century. It bears a simple but profound four-character inscription: "I learn only to be contented". There is a fantastic boiled tofu restaurant on the grounds, which you should be able to find by following the route away from the rock garden and towards the exit. It is slightly expensive, but serves delicious, traditional tofu dishes. The rest of the grounds are worth a look too - particularly the large pond.Admission ¥500.

<u>Ninnaji Temple</u>, (*Nearest bus stop: Omuro Ninnaji, routes 10, 26, 59*), 075-461-1155, . Open daily 9:00 AM - 4:30 PM. Another large temple complex which is often overlooked by tourists. Admission to the grounds is free, allowing visitors to view the 17th century five-story pagoda, and the plantation of dwarf cherry trees (which are always the last to bloom in Kyoto, in early-mid April). Inside the former palace building (which admission is charged to enter) some beautifully painted screen walls are featured, along with a walled garden. In the hills behind the temple, there is a

delightful miniature version of the renowned 88 Temple Pilgrimage in Shikoku, which takes an hour or two (rather than a month or two). This can provide a delightful end to a day of looking at tourist attractions. Walking around the temple grounds is free however, entrance to the former palace building costs ¥500.

Daitokuji Temple, 53 Murasakino (*Nearest bus stop: Daitokuji-mae, routes 28 and 91*), 075-491-0019. A large temple complex, boasting many smaller sub-temples within its grounds. Daitokuji is the quietest of the temples in north-western Kyoto, and if you visit it at the start of the day, you could virtually have it to yourself. Eight of the twenty-four sub-temples are open to the public (most days 9 AM - 5 PM), and each charges an admission fee (around ¥400). The most popular sub-temples are Daisen-in, located on the northern side of the temple complex, which has a beautiful Zen garden, along with delicious cinnamon sweets that only this temple has rights to sell/produce (you can sample one if you get the tea or buy a pack for ¥700), Koto-in particularly noted for its maple trees, which are beautiful in autumn, if you don't mind the crowds, and Hoshun-in which features the same architectural style as Kinkakuji and Ginkakuji Temples as a backdrop to the elegant bridge over a pond.

Imamiya Shrine, 21 Imamiya-cho Murasakino Kita-ku (*Just outside of the Daitokuji complex*), 075-491-0082, . Although the current structure dates back to 1902, the original was built during the Heian Period. At the time, the city was being plagued by illness and disease, so Imamiya Shrine was built to appease the gods. Even today, many visitors come to pray for good health and to ward off illness. Entrance is free.

Tōji-in, (*Nearest bus stop: Tojiin-machi, routes 10 and 26; nearest Randen tram stop, Toji-in*), 075-691-3325. 8 AM to 4:30 PM. Dedicated to the Ashikaga family, the statues inside represent each Ashikaga ruler. The temple also features a lovely garden. Entrance is ¥500.

<u>Hirano Shrine</u>, Hirano Miyamoto-cho, Kita-ku (*Nearest bus stop: Waratenjin-mae, routes 50, 102, 204, 205*), 075-461-4450''", . Open from 6 AM to 5 PM. A small shrine, which is an especially popular destination during the cherry blossom season, setting up amusement and food stalls. A small park of cherry trees next to the shrine is hung with lanterns and drawings by local schoolchildren. Admission is free.

<u>Kitano Tenmangu</u>, (*Nearest bus stop: Kitano Tenmagumae, routes 10 and 50; just east of Kitano Hakubai-Cho, additional routes 101, 102, 204, 205*), 075-461-0005, . Normal hours: 9 AM to 5 PM, on the 25th of every month hours extend from 7 AM to 9 PM. Kitano Tenmangu Shrine was built to appease the soul of Michizane Sugawara, who was a respected member of the Heian Court until he was exiled to Kyushu after falling into disfavor with the Emperor. He died while in exile, and soon after his death, a series of natural disasters mysteriously began plaguing Kyoto. Many suspected that it was the soul of Michizane seeking

vengeance, so in order to console his spirit, he was made the God of Learning, and Kitano Tenmangu was built to honor him. Many plum trees were planted within and around the grounds of the shrine, because they were Michizane's favorite flowers, so this shrine is especially beautiful during the plum blossom season from mid-February to mid-March. The shrine is free to enter, though the treasure house charges a separate ¥300 admission.

<u>Myoshinji Temple</u>, 64 Hanazono Myoshinji-cho, Ukyo-ku (*Nearest bus stop: Myoshin Kitamon-mae, routes 10 and 26. Nearest Randen tram station: Myoshinji*), 075-461-5226, . A large Zen temple complex famous for its large collection of famous artwork. To enter the main hall of Myoshin-ji, you must pay for a tour (tours typically operate every 20 minutes). Inside the main hall you'll find the temple's large dragon painting on the ceiling and the bell. Myoshinji's bell was made in 698, making it one of the oldest in Japan. As one of the head Zen temples, there are many sub-temples on the

temple grounds, each with its own sites and separate fees. Some of the sub-temples are even available for overnight stays and mation (see "Sleep" section). Admission fee: ¥500.

Takao area
While the Takao area offers a modest number of sightseeing opportunities, it is one of Kyoto's most famous places to view the fall leaves. Throughout the autumnal season, the place is quite lively with vendors selling fresh treats and lanterns along the river at night. On the off-season, the area is very quiet, with few tourists. You can see the area in a half-day trip if you wish or stay a little longer to revel in the area's natural beauty (see Momijiya in "Sleep" section for accommodation in the area).

Jingo-ji, (In front of Kyoto Station, take JR Bus bound for Takao/Keihoku and get off at Yamashiro Takao Station (free with JR Pass), walk down a flight of winding stairs, cross a small bridge, and walk up for about ten minutes.). Open9AM-4PM. An overlooked gem among Kyoto temples, it is an ideal place to visit for those wanting to escape the tourist hordes. It is located in Mt. Takao in the north-western corner of Kyoto. Jingoji Temple was established by Priest Kukai as the head of the Shingon Sect during the Heian Period. Make sure you walk all the way to the back of the temple ground to a commanding view of the Kiyotaki River below wedged between two hills; here you can buy clay disks, which you throw down the mountain after making a wish. The temple is especially lovely in the fall, when the leaves all turn colors. Admission fee is ¥500.

<u>Saimyoji Temple</u>. A former sub-temple of Jingoji. While it is not worth making a special trip to see this temple, those touring the Takao area might as well visit, as it is located on the path connecting Jingo-ji to Kozan-ji. The bridge leading to the temple and the lanterns outside the entrance are quite nice. Entrance is free.

<u>Kozan-ji</u>. Registered as one of Kyoto's 17 UNESCO World Heritage Sites, Kozanji is a small temple dating

all the way back to the Kamakura period. Inside the temple you'll find a famous painting of rabbits and monkeys acting as humans, considered to be the world's first manga. Temple grounds are free, entrance to the temple is ¥600.

North-eastern Kyoto
Shimogamo Shrine, 59 Izumigawa-cho, Shimogamo (*From Keihan Demachiyanagi Station, cross the bridge and turn left. Takes about 10 minutes*), 075-781-0010, . Originally built prior to Kyoto becoming Japan's capital, Shimogamo is one of the first shrines built in Kyoto. Together with Kamigamo Shrine, they are known as the Kamo Shrines. These shrines were one of the most revered shrines by the Imperial Court, who made often made offerings here. The forest surrounding the shrine, known as Tadasu no Mori, is believed to be a natural forest, and legend has it that the secrets of those who enter the forest will be revealed. Shimogamo is also a great place to experience Japanese festivals, as many special events are held

here, including the Aoi Matsuri, one of Kyoto's top three festivals. Entrance is free.

<u>Kamigamo Shrine</u>, 3-3-9 Motoyama, 075-781-0011, . Collectively, Kamigamo Shrine and Shimogamo Shrine are known as the Kamo Shrines, and they were highly favored by the Imperial Court during the Heian Period. The shrine is most famous for the *tatesuna*, the two large sand cones. Their origins and original purpose are unknown, but it has been speculated that they represent nearby mountains. Kamigamo Shrine is one of Kyoto's World Heritage Sites. Entrance is free.

<u>Kyoto Botanical Garden</u>. Japan's first botanical garden, the Kyoto Prefectural Botanical Garden is quite large and houses a wide variety of plants. It is a popular place for plum blossom viewing in February and early March and cherry blossoms, which typically bloom in early April. The indoor garden has a wide variety of tropical plants, desert cactuses, and other plants. The entrance fee only covers the outside gardens, but the additional fee to see the garden is quite nominal, so it

is well worth it. ¥200 to see the outdoor flowers and gardens and an additional ¥200 to see the indoor botanical garden.

<u>Shugakuin Imperial Villa</u>, 075-211-1215, . You must make reservations in order to visit Shugakuin. A beautiful villa commissioned by Emperor Gomizuno-o in 1655 and completed four years later. The area is separated into three separate villas. In the lower villa, you'll find a lovely garden with a stream running through it and the Jugetsukan, where the emperor relaxed before making his way to the upper villa. The middle villa is home to the Rakushi-ken, princess Akinomiya's home, and the Kyaku-den, which was also given to Akinomiya when the consort that is was built for died prior to its completion. These buildings contain some particularly beautiful artwork, and an interesting flat pine tree. After seeing all of that, you will finally be escorted to the upper villa. Upon entering the villa, you will ascend the stairs to discover a gorgeous view of the garden and Yokuryu Pond. The tour ends with a

stroll along the outer edges of a pond, past a waterfall and the bridges. Princess Diana was once a guest here, a fact the tour guides love to share with visitors. The best time to visit is said to be the autumn when the leaves are changing. If you plan to visit, make your reservation 3 months in advance for the best chances. Entrance is free.

Entsu-ji. A temple famous for its gardens. A particularly unique feature of this garden is incorporation of Mount Hiei, of which there is a great view from the temple, into the layout of the garden.

Myoman-ji, 91 Hataedacho Iwakura, 075-791-7171, . For anyone looking to see something slightly different from the standard Japanese temple, Myoman-ji offers a replica of Bodh Gaya's Mahabodhi Temple, where the Buddha obtained Enlightenment. The rest of the complex is quite Japanese, but still very beautiful, with artwork and a garden. Temple grounds are free, entrance to the main hall and garden ¥300.

Shisendo, 27 Monguchi-machi, 075-781-2954. Built in 1641, this temple once housed the poet Jozan Ishikawa. Inside the temple there are portraits of 36 influential Chinese poets. Outside there is a garden filled with many azaleas. Entrance is ¥500.

Ohara area

Jakko-in, 075-744-2545, . Open from 9 AM to 5 PM. Built in honor of Prince Shotoku's father, the temple's Jizo contains 6000 tiny Buddha statues inside. The temple is also significant as the final resting place of Empress Kenreimonin, the only member of the Taira clan to survive in the Tales of Heike. Entrance is ¥500.

Sanzen-in, . Open from 8 AM to 5 PM. As the top attraction in the Ohara area, this temple is well worth the visit. Housed within the temple are three ancient Buddha statues. Outside, there is a lovely moss garden and a variety of buddhist statues ranging from the typical spiritual statues to adorable, animated statues. Entrance fee: ¥700.

Raigo-in, 537 Raigo-in-cho, Ohara, 075-744-2161. Open from 9 AM to 5 PM. A temple famous for its Buddhist chants, visitors can hear these chants for free on Sundays at 1 PM. Sutra copying is also offered for ¥1000. Entrance is ¥300.

Amida-ji. A temple where followers are trained to recite the Nyoho Nenbutsu chants. The statue kept within the shrine was originally adorned with the hair of the temple's founding priest.

Shorin-in, 187 Shorinin-machi, 075-744-2409. Open from 9 AM to 5 PM. The priest Honen's famous question-and-answer session was held in the temple's hondo. At the session, he is said to have shined the temple's principal Buddhist sculpture using only his prayers. Entrance is ¥300.

Hosen-in, 187 Shorinin-machi, Ohara, 075-744-2409. Open from 9 AM to 5 PM. Like Yogen-in in Higashiyama, the ceiling of Hosen-in was built using the floorboards of Fushimi Castle, where a bloody historic battle took place. As a result, you'll notice blood stains on the ceiling. Outside, there is a charming garden containing a famous 700 year old pine tree. Entrance is ¥600.

Doing

Zen Mation at Shunko-in, 42 Myoshiji-cho, Hanazono, Ukyo-ku, +81 75 462 5488 9-10:30 AM, 10:40 AM-12:10 PM, 1:30-3 PM daily. The temple's American-educated vice abbot, Rev. Taka Kawakami, offers a detailed English tour of temple and leads Zen mation lessons. The temple hosts many important artistic and cultural properties related to Zen Buddhism and also connected to Shinto and Christianity, and also offers accommodation for ¥5000/night. Accommodations: ¥4000-5000; Tour: ¥2000, including "matcha" green tea and sweet.

Zen Mation at Taizo-in, . Session occurs from 9 AM to 1 PM only one day per week. Much more than simply a Zen mation session, after one hour of mation, participants will also get to experience a brief tea ceremony, calligraphy lessons, and an English tour of the temple's garden. It is a rare opportunity for tourists, but be aware that you will need to devote half of a day for the entire session. Reservations are required, but you can make your reservation in English at the site. All participants must be at least 15 years of age. Cost: ¥7500.

Buying

Kitano Tenmangu Shrine Flea Market. On the 25th of each month Kitano Tenmangu hosts a flea market, with vendors lining both sides of the pathway leading up to the honden and then extends around each side. Pottery, porcelain, traditional dolls, and clothing are among the items sold, along with food. If you can manage to get here on the 25th, it's a great place to find unique souvenirs for great prices.

Eating
Budget

Kurazushi, 4 Hiranomiyajiki-cho (*Between Ryoan-ji and Kinkaku-ji, across from the Inshodomoto Museum of Fine Arts*), 075-466-6101, . Open from 11 AM to 11 PM. A cheap and fun way to dine. For every five plates you finish, put the down the shoot to play a game on the screen above the sushi. Each game is different, but you'll typically be asked to choose one of three options and then watch the animation to see if you win. If you win, you get a prize. It's entertaining, and the sushi tastes good. ¥100 per dish.

Mid-range
Falafel Garden, 3-16 Shimoyanagi-cho, 075-712-1856, . Open from 11:30 AM to 9:30 PM. Closed Wed. in April and May. An Israeli restaurant serving a variety of falafel pockets, as well as meal sets. Medium-sized falafels range in price from ¥860-1100, large sizes available.

Arash's Kitchen, Shōgoin Sannōchō, 4 O Its right across from Kyoto University Hospital`s main entrance, 075-751-5177. Open from 11:30 AM to 10:00 PM.

Everyday. Iranian Restaurant that opened in Feb 2013. Owner is Iranian and works alone. Great place for persian food but also sells falafel and other middle eastern dishes. All the meat is also Halal which is hard to find in Kyoto. Lunch menu is from ¥800-1200 range in price. Dinner is from ¥1000-1800, the portion sizes are large.

Splurge
Matsuno Manryo, 075-701-1577, . Open from noon to 9 PM (last serving at 7:30 PM. An expensive restaurant recommended for those craving high-quality eel, as it is famous for its eel dishes. Prices range from ¥4000-20000. A small bowl of eel soup (considered to be the most famous dish) is ¥5000.

Bistro Cerisier, (*A 4 minute walk from Demachiyanagi Station*), 075-723-5564. Lunch 11:30 AM to 2:30 PM, Dinner 6 PM to 9:30 PM (Closed Wed.). A French restaurant decorated with a variety of French posters. They claim to have the approval of the French themselves. Expect to pay ¥1,000-3,000.

Drinking

Most of the drinking options in the Northern area are located in the Eastern section, within walking distance of Keihan and Eizan Railway stations.

Bar Moonwalk, . Offers a large selection of drinks at a great cost. Finger food is also available. Drinks sell for about ¥200 each, though expect smaller quantities of alcohol than the average bar..

Ringo, 23 Tanakamonzen-cho B1, 075-721-3195, . Open from 5 PM to 3 AM. Closed Mondays. A bar dedicated to the Beatles' singer Ringo Starr, with Beatles memorabilia decorating the walls and even a cover band that plays here live. The fresh pizza is quite good. Cocktails cost ¥400, handmade pizza ¥730.

The Flying Keg (*World Beer Bar*), 6 Tanakasatonomae-cho, Sakyo-ku (*Near Mototanaka Station on the Eizan Line*), 075-701-0245, . Open from 7 PM to 12:30 AM (1 AM on weekends). A great place for anyone wanting to sample beers from around the world or missing beer from home, The Flying Keg offers beers from the U.S.,

Kenya, Germany, Ireland, Israel, China, Mexico, Australia, India, Brazil, Indonesia, Thailand, Belgium, New Zealand, the Caribbean, Italy, and the UK. Most drinks sell for ¥600-900, wines for ¥2000-3000.

<u>Dug Out</u>, 2-24 Shimogamomatsunoki-cho, Sakyo-ku, 075-702-6440, . Open from 5 PM to 2 AM (cafe closes at 9 PM). Closed Tuesdays. A typical bar serving beer, whiskey, tequila, gin, rum, and cocktails. They also offers pizza, pasta dishes, and a variety of appetizers. Most drinks range in price from ¥500-1000.

<u>Kyoto Kamigamo Mankawa</u>, 56-3 Kamigamo Shoubuen-cho, Kita-ku, 075-781-6551, . Open from 5 PM to midnight. Closed Tuesdays and holidays. A cocktail bar along with a restaurant serving various health food dishes. Original cocktails sell for ¥730-840, umeshu ¥630, detox drinks from ¥630-730.

Sleeping

Budget-minded travelers and those escaping the bustle of the urban core may prefer this area. To reach the central city easily, look for connections to the Kitaōji subway station (K04 on the Karasuma line) and bus terminal, the transportation hub of northern Kyoto.

Budget

Temple lodgings

Myōren-ji Temple, Teranouchi Omiya Higashi-iru, Horikawa, Kamigyo-ku (Three minutes by foot from Horikawa Teranouchi Stop on Bus *#9 and 12 - the former leaves from Kyoto Station, the latter from Shijo Karasuma subway station*), +81 (0)75-451-3527. checkin: 6 PM; checkout: 7 AM. Facilities: in-room air-conditioner; no bath but a public bath is nearby; guests should bring their own bath towel and shampoo as the public bath only lends out mini-towels and soap. ¥3800 per person (including entrance fee to public bath).

Myōshin-ji Daishin-in, 57 Myoshinji-cho, Hanazono, Ukyo-ku (10 minutes by foot from Hanazono Station on JR Sagano Line or 7 minutes by foot from Myoshin-ji Mae Stop on buses #8, #10, and #26), +81 (0)75-461-5714 (fax: +81 (0)75-461-5714). 10 rooms with a maximum capacity of 50; in-room air-conditioner, kotatsu heating table in winter, shared bath and toilet. Lights out at 10pm. ¥4700 with breakfast.

<u>Myōshin-ji Shunko-in Temple</u>, 42 Myoshinji-cho, Hanazono, Ukyo-Ku (*Five minutes by foot from the JR Hanazono station, 12-15 minutes away from the JR Kyoto station by JR Sagano Line*), +81 (0)75-462-5488 (), . checkin: 3–7 PM; checkout: noon. The only English available temple accommodation in Kyoto. The guest house has two rooms. A room has a private shower room, toilet, and AC (or a heater). Next to the guest house, there is a fully equipped shared kitchen. The temple hosts many important artistic and cultural properties related to Zen Buddhism, Shinto, and Christianity. One of the properties is the Bell of Nanbanji, which is designated as a national cultural important properties. Call or e-mail for reservation. ¥5,000 per person (including a tour of temple and rental bicycle). Zen mation & tour: ¥2000 (including a bowl of maccha green tea and Japanese sweet)

<u>Myōshin-ji Tōrin-in</u>, 59 Myoshinji-cho, Hanazono, Ukyo-ku (10 minutes by foot from Hanazono Station on JR Sagano Line or 7 minutes by foot from Myoshin-ji Mae Stop on buses #8, #10, and #26), +81 (0)75-463-1334. Only accept reservations from foreigners if they are with a Japanese person. 10 rooms with a maximum capacity of 40; shared bath. Curfew at 9pm. Lights out at 10pm. ¥4700 with breakfast; ¥6000 with breakfast and dinner; Shojin meal (Buddhist vegetarian) ¥3,000–8,000; Shojin cooking class ¥3000.

Hostels

<u>Utano Youth Hostel</u>, 9 Nakayama-cho, Uzumasa, Ukyo-ku (*off Kitaoji-dori*), +81 (0)75-462-2288 (), . checkin: 3:00–11:30 PM; checkout: before 10 AM. Near Ryoanji and Kinkakuji in northwestern Kyoto. There are three bus lines that go out there (26 from Kyoto Station, 10 and 59 from Sanjo-Keihan station) and the stop is right in front of the hostel (Utano Youth Hostel Mae). Bicycle rentals are available and guests are welcome to use the

kitchen, bath and laundry facilities. Dorm room ¥3300, twin ¥4000/person.

Hotels and minshuku
Apical Inn Kyoto, 3-3 Kotakeyabu-Cho Matsugasaki, Sakyo-ku (*Near Shugakuin Station*), 075-722-7711, . checkin: 3:00 PM; checkout: 10:00 AM.

Duo Inn, 3F, 1039-31 Kamiyagawa-cho, Nishi-iru, Onmae, Imakoji-dori, Kamigyo-ku (*About 50 min. from Kyoto Station via #50 bus, or 15 min. walk north from JR Enmachi Station*), +81 (0)75-465-8800 (fax: +81 (0)75-464-1110), . Apartment hotel. Fairly far out in northwest Kyoto but the prices are reasonable. Prices are significantly lower for stays of 7 or more nights. Payment by cash only. No daily cleaning and no bath towels provided. Bus journey from Kyoto Station takes about 50 minutes. Singles ¥6300, doubles ¥8400–10,500, triples ¥12,600, 2-4 person Japanese-style room ¥14,700.

GuestHouse Bon, 63-2 Kamimonzen-cho Murasakino, Kita-ku (*8 min. west of Kitaōji subway station K04, north exit*), +81 (0)75-493-2337, . checkin: 3–10 PM; checkout: 11 AM. Located in northwest Kyoto, immediately east of Daitokuji. Inexpensive bicycle rentals. The guest house owner has lived in Western countries before and can speak fluent English and a pinch of Spanish. All Japanese-style rooms, but can be converted to dorm style upon request for larger parties. Singles ¥3800–4500, doubles ¥4500–6000, triples ¥7500.

Hotel Chrysantheme, 51, Hirano Kamihatcho Yanagimachi, Kita-ku (*near Ritsumeikan University, 30 min. from Kyoto Station via buses #50 or 205*), +81 (0)75-462-1540 (fax: +81 (0)75-462-1571), . checkin: 2–9 PM; checkout: 11 AM. Western-style rooms with shower and bath shared between every two rooms. Also oriented towards the longer-stay market, with discounts starting at 5 days and increasing through 30. Singles ¥4800, doubles ¥9600 (without long-stay discounts).

Midrange

Holiday Inn Kyoto, 36 Takano, Nishihiraki-cho, Sakyo-ku, Kyoto 606-8103 (*Several minutes away on foot from the Takanobashi-higashizume bus stop*), 075-721-3131 (fax: 075-781-6178), . checkin: 14:00; checkout: 12:00. The hotel runs a scheduled shuttle service to and from Kyoto Station for its guests. Rates start at ¥10000.

Momijiya, Takao Umegahata, Ukyo-ku, 075-871-1005, . Although this hotel operates year round, it is extremely popular in the autumn ("momiji" is the Japanese term for the changing of leaves). It is located in the quiet, far northeastern area of Takao near the foot of the stairway leading to Jingo-ji. It makes for a nice retreat, and you can opt to stay in a room with an open-air bath to relax while you enjoy the natural surroundings. All rooms are designed for at least 2 people. Prices start from ¥14700.

Splurge
Grand Prince Hotel Kyoto, 1092-2 Iwakura-Hataeda-cho, Sakyo-ku (*Nearest station: Kokusai Kaikan on the*

Subway Karasuma Line. Takagaraike Park is adjacent to the hotel), 075-712-1111. checkin: 1:00 PM; checkout: 12:00 PM. Prices vary greatly from ¥11000-45000, depending on the room.

Kyoto South.

Southern Kyoto covers a large part of Japan's former capital, stretching from the Ōharano area in the west to Fushimi-ku, Daigo, and the southern tip of Higashiyama-ku in the east. The ancient city of Uji borders the district to the southeast.

Some of the district's better-known attractions include Daigo-ji - which is inscribed as a World Heritage Site within the group "Historic Monuments of Ancient Kyoto" - and the seemingly endless lines of torii stretching up the mountainside above Fushimi-Inari Shrine.

Getting in
By train

Originating from the city's main transport hub at Kyoto Station, the JR Nara Line is a convenient link for tourists travelling between Central and Southeastern Kyoto. Trains running on the Keihan Main Line fulfill a similar role, connecting Eastern Kyoto to the south (although they do *not* stop at Kyoto Station). JR Inari Station and Keihan Fushimi-Inari Station both put visitors almost at the doorstep of the Fushimi-Inari Shrine, one of the district's most famous attractions. The Keihan Line also provides easy access for those continuing on to U ji or Hirakata.

By subway
From Central and Eastern Kyoto, the municipal subway system's Tōzai Line goes as far south as Rokujizō Station where passengers can transfer to the JR Nara Line. The Tōzai Line stations Ono and Daigo bring travellers within reach of Zuishin-in and Daigo-ji, respectively.

By bus

To get to the Fushimi area by bus, take Bus 5 South (南5) to reach Tofukuji (Tofukuji-michi) and Fushimi Inari Taisha (Inari Taisha-mae). Make sure you are on the South bus; the other number 5 bus will take you the opposite direction (through Higashiyama all the way to Northern Kyoto).

There are no direct buses to the Oharano area, so it's best to travel via Hankyu Railway to Higashimuko Station. From here, you can then take the Hankyu Bus to get closer to other attractions.

Seeing
Southeast
Fushimi Inari Taisha, (*Keihan Main Line train to Fushimi-Inari Station or JR Nara Line to Inari Station*), +81-075-641-7331, . Another of Kyoto's often-overlooked jewels, located just south of Higashiyama in the Fushimi area. Dedicated to Inari, the Japanese fox goddess, Fushimi-Inari-taisha is the head shrine (*taisha*) for 40,000 Inari shrines across Japan. Stretching 230 meters up the hill behind it are

hundreds of bright red *torii* (gates). A visitor could easily spend several hours walking up the hillside, taking in the beautiful views of the city of Kyoto and walking through the *torii*, which appear luminescent in the late afternoon sun. Countless stone foxes, also referred to as Inari, are also dotted along the path. Watch your fingers as you go - the fox spirits are said to be able to possess people by slipping through their fingernails. Admission is free.

Fushimi Momoyama Castle. This castle was once a favorite of Toyotomi Hideyoshi. The original was dismantled in 1623, but a 1964 reconstruction went up in its memory with a small museum and gold-lined tea room.

Teradaya. Open from 10 AM to 4:00 PM. It was here at this inn where Ryoma Sakamoto, a famous samurai who wanted to overthrow the Tokugawa, was injured in an attack, although he escaped. Some pictures, his handgun, and other historical artifacts are viewable inside. Entrance is ¥400.

Tōfuku-ji, 075-541-2565, . Open from 9 AM to 4 PM. A large temple complex with many small and beautiful gardens nearby. Hordes of Japanese tourists visit during the fall months, when the leaves show a dazzling array of colors, but it's not as well known to foreigners. A pleasant side path through the woods connects it to the Fushimi Inari grounds.

Jonangu Shrine, 7 Nakashima Tobarikyu-cho, Fushimi-ku, 075-623-0846, . Open from 9 AM to 4:30 PM. Although Jonangu Shrine is rarely visited by foreign tourists, it is a beautiful shrine with extensive history. It was originally established by Emperor Kammu when Kyoto became the nation's capital. At the end of the Heian period, it became home to retired emperor Goshirakawa. As a result, the beautiful Rakusui-en Garden was constructed. As a former Imperial Villa, Jonangu Shrine is a great alternative for those who are unable to secure reservations to Shugakuin or Katsura Imperial Villas, because no reservations are required to enter Jonangu Shrine's garden. Entrance to the shrine grounds is free, but the garden costs ¥500 to enter.

Daigō-ji, 22 Higashioji-cho, Daigo, 075-571-0002, . The Garan and Sanboin are open from 9 AM to 5 PM from March through November, and 9 AM to 4 PM from December through February. The museum is open from 9 AM to 4 PM. Daigoji is a large temple complex consisting of the garan (main complex), Sanboin Garden, and Reihokan Museum. The size and position of the temple, slightly removed from the city, creates a more peaceful, serene setting. As a registered World Heritage Site, the temple has a lot of history, with the oldest remaining structure being the five-story pagoda built in 951. The Sanboin is the temple's garden, and despite being rather pricey is truly beautiful.

The museum houses many of the temple's treasures. Daigoji Temple is famous for being one of Kyoto's best places to view cherry blossoms in the spring and the leaves in the fall. Although the main temple complex is always worth visiting, those visiting in the autumn should consider paying the extra fee to see the Sanboin garden, as it becomes especially beautiful with the vivid colors of the leaves (sadly pictures are not allowed in the Sanboin). Daigō-ji is a 1.1 km (0.7 mi) walk from the Daigō subway station (Tozai Line). Alternatively, the Yamakyu Keihan Bus line departs directly from Kyoto Station near the Hachijo exit for ¥300 each way. Timetable (pdf, Japanese only) Each part costs ¥600 to enter however discount tickets can be purchased to see two (¥1000) or all three (¥1500).

Zuishin-in, 075-571-0025, . 9 AM to 4:30 PM. According to legend, this is where Ono no Komachi, one of Japan's famous femme fatales, resided. She made Prince Fukakusa agree to court her for 100 days before she would agree to marry him, but on the 99th day, he died, leaving her single and her beauty to fade. Entrance is ¥400.

Kaju-ji, 27-6 Kanshujiniodo-cho, Yamashina-ku (*Nearest station: Subway Tozai Line's One Station*), 075-571-0048. Open from 9 AM to 4 PM. A temple with a peaceful lilly pond and a variety of cherry trees. Admission: ¥400.

Video game giant Nintendo has its world headquarters in southern Kyoto. Sad to say, tours are not offered, and visitors are unlikely even to make it into the lobby; the best you'll be able to do is pose for a photo with the company logo on the plaza in front of the otherwise anonymous building.

Oharano area
The Oharano area, located in the Southwest, is named after Oharano Shrine, one of the most famous sites in the area. While it is not really so far from the inner city, it does not reflect any of the stereotypical images one has when they think of Kyoto. The area is so rural, it feels as though the nearest city is hundreds of miles away. Most tourists are not even aware this area exists, so it can be a nice change of pace for those who have the time to explore the outer regions.

<u>Oharano Shrine</u>, 1152 Minami Kasuga-cho Oharano, 075-331-0014, . Always open. The shrine is believed to

have been moved to Nagaokakyo at the bidding of Empress Kammu, who made it the shrine of the Fujiwara family's guardian god. The Imperial Court made annual offerings at this shrine. The pond within the shrine precincts was once a popular place for writing poetry. Because the area is removed from the inner city, the shrine is quite peaceful; it is not unusual to have the entire place to yourself. Entrance is free.

Shōbō-ji, 1102 Kasuga-cho Oharano (*Located on the opposite side of the road as Oharano Shrine*), 075-331-0105. Open from 9 AM to 5 PM. A Shingon sect temple featuring an impressive statue of the 3-faced thousand armed Kannon and a beautiful, well-kept Zen rock garden. Many of the rocks within the garden were chosen to resemble animals, like a rabbit and frog. Entrance is ¥300.

Shoji-ji, 1194 Minamikasuga-cho Oharano, 075-331-0601. Open from 9 AM to 4:30 PM. Nicknamed Cherry Blossom Temple (*hana no tera*), it hosts a beautiful display of blossoms in the spring. Entrance is ¥400.

Yoshimine-dera, 1372 Oshio-cho, Oharano, 075-331-0020, . Open from 8 AM to 5 PM. In 1034 Emperor Go-Ichijo gave Yoshimine-dera imperial rank, so the head priest was a member of the imperial family for many years, although it is no longer so today. The 20th temple on the Saigoku Kannon Pilgrimage. Entrance fee: ¥400 (¥500 during special exhibit).

Doing

JRA Kyoto Racecourse, 32 Yoshijima-Watashibajima-cho, Fushimi-ku (*just outside Keihan Yodo Station*), . For those interested in horse races, Kyoto's racecourse is the mecca of horseracing in the Kansai area.

Riverboat Cruises, 075-623-1030, . Call to make a reservation to schedule your ride. No tours are offered on Mondays. A peaceful ride down the canal past all of the historic sake breweries. It's a unique experience. Costs ¥4100 for adults, ¥2700 for elementary school and younger.

Buying

Ryomakan, Chuou Ryoma-dori, 075-602-2550, . Open from 10 AM to 5 PM. An interesting souvenir shop dedicated to the famous samurai Ryoma Sakamoto. Inside you'll find some of the typical tourist souvenirs, like Ryoma Sakamoto keychains, but there are also some interesting and unique finds. Those looking to purchase swords may find that this shop sells more authentic swords than those in Kyoto's larger tourist spots.

Eating

Local delicacies are sold at the roadside approaching Fushimi-Inari Shrine, including barbecued sparrow and *inarizushi* (sweetened sushi rice wrapped in fried tofu), which is said to be the favourite food of the fox. The *suzume* is still in a form that resembles the animal (essentially a barbecued bird on a skewer), so those not accustomed may be a bit squeamish. If you plan to walk the path around Fushimi Inari and you wish to sample inarizushi, you can save money by stopping at the small restaurant up the path within the grounds of the shrine. It also provides a great view of a line of the torii gates from above.

<u>Usagiya</u>, (*near Subway Tozai Line's Ono Station*), 075-573-5523, . Open from 5:30 PM to 11:30 PM (Closed Mon.). Serves a variety of delicious ramen dishes. Ramen sells for ¥900.

<u>Uosaburo</u>, (*Just outside Keihan Fushimi Momoyama Station*), 075-601-0061, . Open from 11 AM to 10 PM. A pricey restaurant serving local Kyoto cuisine with a variety of set options. From ¥7000-25000.

Torisei, 075-622-5533, . Open from 11:30 AM to 11 PM. Closed Mon. Serves a variety of chicken and meat dishes. Individual portions from ¥500-730.

<u>Kyozu-an (Fushimi Inari branch)</u>, 16-20 Fukakusa-hatsugawa-cho, Fushimi-ku 〒612-0013 , 075-641-1887, . 10-6. Located on the bustling street connecting the Keihan Fushimi-Inari and JR Inari stations, this shop sells soft-serve ice cream made with soy milk. The

resulting texture is creamier than regular soft-serve ice cream, and famously allows the cone to be held upside down without the ice cream falling out. Available in matcha, vanilla, and other seasonal flavors. ¥300+.

Drinking

Gekkeikan, 247 Minamihama-cho, Fushimi-ku, 075-623-2056, . Open from 9:30 AM to 4:30 PM Tues.-Sun. Founded in 1637, this local sake brewing company remains popular among Japanese even today. Many of the old breweries still exist and visitors can tour Gekkeikan and visit the attached museum to get a glimpse of how the sake is made. Entrance fee: ¥300.

Getting in to Kyoto

By plane
Kyoto does not have its own airport, but rather is served by Osaka's two airports. There is an excellent road and railway network between the two cities.

From Kansai

By train

Overseas travellers can fly into Kansai International Airport and then get a train to Kyoto. Kansai Airport Station is located opposite the arrival lobby where the Japanese Rail (JR) West Haruka Kansai Airport Limited Express Train can be caught. The best and fastest way to get to Kyoto from the airport is to buy a one-day JR West Kansai Area Pass and take the Haruka Limited Express (non-reserved tickets only). The Haruka Limited Express takes about 77 minutes, with trains leaving every 30-60 minutes. The pass is for foreigners only and costs ¥2,300, which is ¥680 less than a regular Haruka Limited Express ticket from the airport to Kyoto. You will need to show your passport, as well as a copy of your foreign-bound return flight, when purchasing a ticket.

Another option that JR started to offer is the ICOCA and HARUKA discount ticket which includes travel in unreserved seating on the Haruka to Kyoto and any JR station within a designated "Free Zone" and a rechargeable ICOCA transit card containing ¥2000 (includes ¥500 deposit) that can be used on JR, private railways, buses and stores in the Kansai region. A one-way discount ticket costs ¥1600 and a round-trip costs ¥3200.

Both of the above tickets can be purchased online or at the Kansai Airport train station.

By bus

Comfortable limousine buses run from the airport to Kyoto Station, twice an hour, stopping at some of the major hotels along the way. The ticket costs ¥2,500 (children ¥1,250) one-way or ¥4,000 for round-trip. Bus tickets can be purchased outside of the airport's arrival lobby on the first floor. (just go straight when you leave customs through the "North gate"). The buses leave from bus stop #8, which is located directly opposite the ticket vending machine. The ride takes 88 minutes but can take longer when there is traffic (about 90 135 minutes).

From Itami

Located near Osaka, Itami Airport is Kansai's largest domestic airport. Travelers flying into Kyoto from other areas in Japan will most likely arrive here. The easiest way to get to Kyoto from Itami Airport is by limousine bus No. 15. The trip takes about an hour and costs ¥1,280. The buses run three times an hour. Alternatively, you can take a combination of monorail and train, which requires at least two changes (monorail to Hotarugaike, Hankyu Takarazuka Line to Juso, Hankyu Kyoto Line to Kyoto) but costs just ¥650 and can be completed in an hour. Whereas the Limousine Bus will leave you at Kyoto Station in the southern part of Kyoto, the Hankyu Railway runs to Shijō Street in central Kyoto.

By train

Most visitors arrive at JR Kyoto station by Shinkansen (bullet train) from Tokyo. *Nozomi* trains take approximately 2.15 hrs. to Kyoto and costs ¥13520 one-way. Travel agencies in Tokyo and Kyoto sell nozomi tickets with ¥700-1,000 discount. If you buy a ticket in an agency, it is "open date" - you can board any train as long as it is not full. All you have to do is show up at the train station, register your agency ticket and then you will be reserved a seat. The trains are equipped with vending machines and attendants selling snacks. *Hikari* trains, which run less frequently and make a few more stops, cover the trip in around 2.45 hours, but only the *Hikari* and the *Kodama* trains can be used by Japan Rail Pass holders at no charge.

Travelers can also take advantage of the Puratto Kodama Ticket, which offers a discount on the all-stopping Kodama services if purchased at least one day in advance. You get a reserved seat and a free drink on board. With this ticket a trip from Tokyo to Kyoto costs ¥9800 and takes 3.45 hours. Note that there is only one Kodama service per hour from Tokyo, and a few early-morning Kodama trains cannot be used with this ticket.

During travel periods when the Seishun 18 Ticket is valid, you can go from Tokyo to Kyoto during the day in about 8.30 hours using all-local trains. Traveling in a group is the best way to get discounts. The usual fare is ¥8000 however a party of three costs ¥3800 per person, and a group of five traveling together drops the price down to ¥2300 per person.

For travel in the Kansai region, a cheaper and almost as fast alternative is the JR *shinkaisoku* rapid service, which connects to Osaka, Kobe and Himeji at the price of a local train. For a slightly cheaper price you can use the private Hankyu or Keihan lines to Osaka and Kobe, or the Kintetsu line to Nara. The Kansai Thru Pass includes travel on the private lines through to Kyoto, and this may prove cheaper that a JR Pass if you are staying a few days in the area.

Overnight by train
Direct overnight train service between Tokyo and Kyoto on a daily basis was abolished with the discontinuation of the *Ginga* express train in 2008. An

alternative route via northern Japan became moot when another overnight train was removed from regular service in 2012. As a result, taking the bus is now the easiest way to travel between these two cities at night.

Overnight travel between Tokyo and Kyoto is still possible, and if you have a Japan Rail Pass and are willing to do some research, it can be inexpensive as well. The idea is to split your journey into two parts, stopping at an intermediate destination en-route in order to sleep somewhere. Your cost will only be for the hotel room, as your train fare has already been paid for on your rail pass.

This two-part method carries a couple of advantages: location and money. You will more than likely find good accomodations very close to a main train station in a smaller city, compared to a big city such as Tokyo, and it will more than likely be cheaper than hotels found in Tokyo. You could use the money you save to forward some of your luggage to Kyoto using a luggage delivery service and take an overnight bag with you, which will make the journey easier.

For example, you can use the Tokaido Shinkansen late at night and sleep over at a hotel in Shizuoka, Hamamatsu, Toyohashi or Nagoya; In the morning, grab one of the first bullet train departures in the same direction to continue your trip. Here is an example: In the evening hours, take a *Hikari* or *Kodama*train to Hamamatsu (75-90 minutes via *Hikari* or 2 hours via *Kodama*). Once there you can take a rest at Hamamatsu's Toyoko Inn, which costs as low as ¥4000 for a single room if booked in advance. At 6:30 the next morning, board the first bullet train of the day, a Kodama, and you will be in Kyoto before 8:00.

Remember that Japan Rail Passes are also valid for JR buses operating between Tokyo and Kyoto (see 'By Bus').

By car
Kyoto is easily reached by car via the Meishin Expressway between Nagoya and Osaka, but you'll

definitely want to park your car on the outskirts of the city and use public transport to get around. Most attractions are in places built well before the existence of automobiles, and the availability of parking varies between extremely limited and non-existent. Furthermore, what little parking is available might be outrageously expensive.

By bus

As Kyoto is a major city, there are many day and overnight buses which run between Kyoto and other locations throughout Japan, which can be a cheaper alternative than shinkansen fares.

The run between Tokyo and the Kansai region is the busiest in Japan, and fierce competition between bus operators has resulted in better amenities and lower prices. Buses from Tokyo follow either the Tomei Expressway or the Chuo Expressway to Nagoya, then the Meishin Expressway to Kyoto. Trips take approximately 7-9 hours depending on the route and stops.

The following are among the major bus services available between Tokyo and Kyoto: *(Current as of March, 2012)*

Willer Express

Discount bus operator Willer Express runs daytime and overnight buses with a variety of seating options ranging from standard bus seats to luxurious shell seats. Bus journeys can be booked online in English, and Willer's Japan Bus Pass is valid on all of their routes with some exceptions.

Buses from Tokyo leave from Willer's own bus terminal, located west of Shinjuku Station in the Sumitomo Building. Some buses also leave from Tokyo Disneyland - Goofy Car Park, Tokyo Station - Yaesu-Chuo Exit, Shinagawa Station - Shinagawa Prince Hotel and Yokohama Station. In Kyoto, Willer Express uses the Hachijo Exit at the south side of Kyoto Station, with some routes also stopping in front of the Kiyomizu-Gojo post office.

Willer's overnight one-way fares to/from Tokyo start from approximately ¥3800 for overnight trips in standard seats up to ¥9800 in shell seats with advanced purchase. Daytime bus fares start from ¥4900. Fares are typically higher on weekends and holidays.

JR Bus

JR Bus is also a major operator on the Tokyo-Kyoto route. The drawback is that you cannot make online reservations in English, but you can make reservations in train stations at the same "Midori-no-Madoguchi" ticket windows used to reserve seats on trains.

JR Buses depart from Tokyo Station - Yaesu Exit and the JR Highway Bus Terminal located adjacent to Yoyogi Station on the Yamanote Line (one stop south of Shinjuku). In Kyoto, buses congregate at the Karasuma Exit at the north side of Kyoto Station.

JR Bus offers, in order of comfort and price, Seishun (youth) buses with 2x2 seating configurations, Standard buses with individual seats arranged 1x1x1, and Premium Buses that offer wider seats and more amenities.

JR Bus' overnight one-way fares to/from Tokyo start from approximately ¥3500 for overnight trips in Seishun buses up to ¥7600 for premium buses with advanced purchase. Daytime bus fares start from ¥5000. Fares are typically higher on weekends and holidays.

Some JR Buses heading to/from Osaka stop at the Kyoto Fukakusa Bus Stop on the Meishin Expressway. Fujinomori Station on the Keihan Railway is a 10-minute walk from Fukakusa, while Takeda Station on the Kintetsu Railway and the Kyoto Subway is 15 minutes away; all can be used to reach the main city. A local city bus also runs to Kyoto station from the nearby Youth Science Center 1-2 times per hour.

Note that the Japan Rail Pass CAN be used for overnight trips on standard buses between Tokyo and Kyoto called "Dream" services. If traveling during the daytime, direct buses between Tokyo and Kyoto are NOT covered by the rail pass (you can use the much faster bullet train instead).

Other bus services

Hankyu Bus: overnight from Ikebukuro Station, Shinagawa Bus Terminal and Yokohama Station. Fares start from ¥7950. Buses stop at the Kyoto New Hankyu Hotel.

Keihan Bus: overnight from Shinjuku Highway Bus Terminal, Shibuya Mark City, Tokyo Disneyland and Keisei Ueno station. Discount buses ¥5000; regular buses ¥8180. Buses stop at Kyoto Station's Hachijo Exit.

Kintetsu Bus: overnight from Asakusa Station, Ueno Station, Tokyo Station and Yokohama Station. "Flying Liner" buses from ¥6320; "Flying Sneaker" discount bus from ¥3900 with advance purchase. Buses stop at Kyoto Station's Hachijo Exit.

Kosoku Bus: overnght from Shinjuku station, Tokyo station (Yaesu South exit, Kajibashi Parking Lot), and other places. The cheapest ticket is ¥1800. The buses arrives to Jujo Kanagawa (close to Jujo subway station).

Getting around

The sheer size of the city of Kyoto, and the distribution of tourist attractions around the periphery of the city, make the city's public transport system invaluable.

One of the easiest ways to plan a route is through Hyperdia or Kurage. These sites contain station-to-station route plans, which reference public and private trains and subways as well as buses throughout Japan.

If you are planning to travel beyond city limits you might consider using the tickets from Surutto Kansai. For use in west Japan, including Kyoto, there are some other useful tickets: a rechargeable smart card, ICOCA, can be used on rail, subway and bus networks in the Kansai area and also Okayama, Hiroshima, Nagoya (Kintetsu trains) and Tokyo (JR East trains). These cards are available at vending machines at these rail stations, and cost ¥2000, which includes a ¥500 deposit that will be refunded when the card is returned at JR West Station. For use in Kyoto only there are some other useful tickets:

The Kyoto Sightseeing Card can be purchased as a one-day (Adults ¥1200/Children ¥600) or two-day pass (¥2000/¥1000). It can be used for unlimited travel on the subway and city buses as well as a part of the Kyoto bus route. The two-day pass has to be used on two consecutive days. This can be purchased in the Kyoto tourist information in Kyoto station, near the entrance to the subway.

The Traffica Kyoto Card is a stored-value card in denominations of ¥1000 or ¥3000. It can be conveniently used up to face value on all subways and buses by simply sliding it through the ticket gate. They offer a 10% bonus value.

By train

Kyoto is criss-crossed by several train lines, all of which are clearly sign-posted in English. Although the lines are run independently and prices vary slightly between them, transfers can be purchased at most of the ticket machines. The Keihan train line can be useful for traveling in eastern Kyoto, while the two Keifuku tram lines are an attractive way of traveling in the northwest. Across the street from the northern terminus of the Keihan Line is the Eidan Eizan line, which runs to Mount Hiei and Kurama. The Hankyu Line starts at *Shijo-Kawaramachi* downtown, and connects to the Karasuma Line one stop later at *Karasuma*. It's useful for reaching *Arashiyama* and the *Katsura Rikyu*; it runs all the way to Osaka and Kobe. JR lines run from Kyoto station to the northwest (JR Sagano line), to the southwest (JR Kyoto line) and to the southeast (JR Nara line). There are local and express trains so check if they stop at your station before you get on.

By subway
There are two subway lines which only serve a rather small part of the city. The north-south running Karasuma Line runs under Kyoto Station, and the west-

east running Tozai Line links up with it near the city center. Both are useful for travel in the city center but not really suitable for temple-hopping. The Tozai Line does connect with the Keihan Line, however, which runs parallel to the Kamo-gawa, and is convenient for reaching *Gion* and southern Kyoto; it also gets you within a short walk of many of the sights in eastern Kyoto.

A one-day pass for the subway costs ¥ 600.

By bus

The bus network is the only practical way of reaching some attractions, particularly those in north-western Kyoto. Fortunately the system is geared toward tourists, with destinations electronically displayed/announced in English as well as Japanese. Unlike other Japanese cities, a tourist probably is advised to use the buses here.

Confusingly however, there are two different bus companies in Kyoto, which occasionally even have overlapping line numbers. Green-and-white Kyoto City

Buses travel within the city, and are the most useful for visitors; unless otherwise noted, all buses listed in this guide are city buses. Red-and-white Kyoto Buses travel to the suburbs and are generally much less useful.

Many buses depart from Kyoto Station, but there are well-served bus stations closer to the city center at Sanjo-Kawabata just outside the Sanjo Keihan subway line, and in the northern part of the city at the Kitaoji subway station. Most city buses have a fixed fare of ¥230, which is paid into a box next to the driver when getting off. Exact change is required, but machines for exchanging coins and ¥1000 notes are available. You can also purchase a one-day pass (¥600 for adults and ¥250 for children under 12) with which you can ride an unlimited number of times within a one day period. The day passes can be bought from the bus drivers or from the bus information center just outside Kyoto Station. This is especially useful if you plan on visiting many different points of interest within Kyoto. You can also buy a combined unlimited subway and bus 1-day pass for ¥1200 and slightly more economical 2-day pass for ¥2000. Note that these passes are not valid on JR trains and busses that serve the area.

The municipal transport company publishes a very useful leaflet called Bus Navi. It contains a route map for the bus lines to most sights and fare information. You can pick it up at the information center in front of the main station.

Raku Bus - The city has three routes (100, 101, and 102) which are specifically designed for foreign tourists wishing to hit the tourist spots quickly. The buses skip many of the non-tourist stops and are thus a faster way to get from one sight to the next. The Raku Bus leaves from platform D2 at Kyoto Station. The cost is ¥220 per ride, but the day passes are accepted as well.

By bicycle

Particularly in spring and fall, but at any time of year, getting around by bicycle is an excellent option. Cycling forms a major form of personal transport year-round for locals. The city's grid layout makes navigation easy.

You can rent bicycles in many places in Japan for a reasonable price. During the peak tourist seasons, when roads are busy and buses tend to be crammed beyond capacity, bicycles are probably the best way to navigate Kyoto.

Kyoto's wide, straight roads make for heavy traffic in many parts of the city, but it is possible to find back alleys that are quieter and offer better chances to happen upon all sorts of sightseeing/cultural gems. Riding on major roads is OK, especially if you are confident and used to riding with traffic on the road, rather than on the sidewalk and especially again if you are used to riding/driving on the LEFT-HAND side of the road.

Kyoto Cycling Tour Project(KCTP), 075-354-3636. A five-minute walk from the North Exit (the side with the buses and Kyoto Tower) of Kyoto Station. Bikes range from ¥ 1000 to ¥ 2000 for an actual 27-speed mountain bike with city-tires on it; perfect for the average foreigner who is used to a 'real' bike in their home country. The following options can be added: bi-lingual cycling/walking map of Kyoto ¥ 100; light FREE; helmet ¥ 200; back pack; ¥ 100; rain poncho ¥ 100. They can hold on to your luggage while you are riding.

There are four other locations of KCTP and you can return your bike to any location, however you will incur a ¥ 400 charge if you return the bike to a location other than the one you rented from. Guided bike tours are also available ranging from ¥ 4500 (three hours) to ¥ 13000 (7.5 hours) that include guide, bike rental, lunch/snacks, accident insurance and admission to some attractions on the tour. Minimum of two people to guarantee departure/maximum of 10. Needs to be reserved three days in advance if you want a tour. Don't worry if the mountain bikes sell out - Kyoto (like Tokyo) is a city with perfect kerb transitions so a 3 speed with basket and bell is fine, if a little bumpy on the river path.

There is a friendly bicycle rental shop across the street from the Keihan Demachiyanagi station, behind the taxi rank. ¥ 500 for a day, ¥ 750 for a day and night, and ¥ 3000 for a month. ¥ 3000 deposit (¥ 2000 when showing ID). Has 22" children's bikes which come with a free helmet. Opens early (9AM) - 7PM.

There is a small rental shop just north of Sanjo Keihan station on Kawabata Dori that rents bicycles, which doesn't have "tourist signs" attached. On the downside, they do not speak English. ¥ 1000 per day.

Rakusaiguchi, Katsura, and Saiin stations have Hankyu rent-a-cycle locations, where bikes can be rented for 320 yen a day, and returned the next morning. Electrically assisted bicycles are also available for 430 yen.

For those staying more than a week or so, purchasing a used bicycle may be economical. Most bicycle shops in Kyoto offer used town bicycles with lights, bell, basket, and lock for around ¥ 5000 ¥ 10,000 (plus a ¥ 500 registration fee). At least some of this cost can be made back by re-selling the bicycle just prior to departure. Cycle Eirin, a chain found throughout the city, is a good place to start.

Seeing

Kyoto offers an incredible number of attractions for tourists, and visitors will probably need to plan an itinerary in advance in order to visit as many as possible.

Japan National Tourist Organization's self-guided "Kyoto Walks" pamphlet is available in a ready to print PDF format here. The guide enables first time visitors to tour the city with ease and with minimum fuss by providing bus numbers, names of bus stops and clearly marked walking routes. There are a variety of self-guided walks in different districts to sample Kyoto's various sites. If you see the browser's dialog box popping up, just click on it till the entire PDF document opens.

World Heritage Site

In 1994, 17 historic sites were inscribed on UNESCO's World Heritage List under the group designation Historic Monuments of Ancient Kyoto. Fourteen of the listed sites are in Kyoto itself, two are in the neighbouring city of Uji and one is in Ōtsu.

Imperial Palaces and Villas

Stroll through the regal retreats of the Imperial Palace or one of the two Imperial villas with gardens and teahouses managed by the Imperial Household Agency. These are the Imperial Palace and Sentō Imperial Palace in Central Kyoto, Katsura Imperial Villa in Western Kyoto, and Shugakuin Imperial Villa in Northern Kyoto. All four of these sites are open to the public by reservation through the Imperial Household Agency. The gardens located within the precincts of each palace and villa are at their most scenic during spring cherry blossom season and autumn where a riot of colors enchant visitors. Each property is still used from time to time for official state functions or for private visits by the current royal family members.

The Imperial Household Agency maintains a quota on the number of visitors to each site per tour. Admission is free. English guides are available at the Imperial Palace; however, tours of the Sento Imperial Palace, Katsura Villa, and Shugakuin Villa are conducted in Japanese only (English pamphlets are given at each destination upon entry and books are available for purchase if you'd like to know more). Overseas visitors can apply online to the Imperial Household Agency in English here. On its site are write ups and videos in English for interested visitors to gauge which ones they would like to visit before making an online application.

Please note that advanced applications first become available on the first day of the month, three months in advance of the applicant's preferred touring month. For example, if your preferred date of visit falls in the month of April, you can begin applying on January 1. As these visits are over subscribed by the Japanese and overseas visitors, the Imperial Household Agency has to draw lots to pick the successful applicants. All applicants are notified on the status of their applications whether they are successful or otherwise within a week after closing date. Most applicants to the Imperial Palace are accepted, and early reservation is not usually necessary; however, those planning to visit the Sentō Imperial Palace, or either of the Imperial Villas should apply on the first available day of application as they are highly competitive and entire months of tours often become full within the first few days. Winter tours are typically much less competitive, but be aware that the gardens will not be as beautiful as other times of the year.

If an applicant is not successful, they can still go direct in person to the Imperial Household Agency Kyoto Office to enquire whether there are vacancies, as they typically save a few spots for walk-ins. Many people are able to do this successfully for the Imperial Palace, but it can be more of a risk for the others, so go early. Address: Imperial household Agency Kyoto Office, 3

Kyotogyoen, Kamigyo-ku, Kyoto, 602-8611, tel: +81-75-211-1215.

Doing

Public baths

Public baths have been a cornerstone of the society for centuries in Kyoto. The first public baths, or sentō, were documented in the 13th century. Soon they became one of the few places in society where social status was irrelevant. Noblemen shared baths with commoners and warriors. Today over 140 bath houses remain in Kyoto. Funaoka Onsen is the oldest of these and dubbed "king of sentō", but newer bath houses and super sentō are just as much part of the Japanese bathing culture. If you have the time, make your way to one of the many public bath houses Kyoto has to offer.

Funaoka Onsen, Kyoto, Kita Ward, Murasakino Minamifunaokacho 82-1 (*take bus line 206 from Kyoto station*), +81-75-441-3735. 15:00 - 01:00. Funaoka Onsen is the oldest public bath house in Kyoto still in operation. Its classic building is an excellent example of bath house architecture of the beginning of the 20th century. Funaoka Onsen is popular with both locals and visitors and is a must if you have an hour to spare. ¥430.

Mation

Well-known for its abundance of historical sites, Kyoto often draws visitors eager to experience traditional Japanese culture. Buddhist mation sessions are one of the most popular of these activities, and multiple options are available. In Northern Kyoto, Taizo-in and Shunko-in (both sub-temples of Myoshin-ji) offer authentic Zen mation sessions, complete with explanations of the meaning and significance of such mation. Reservations are necessary.

Blossom Viewing

Cherry blossoms

Kyoto is arguably the most well known place in the country to view cherry blossoms, and there are certainly no lack of options. On the Official Top 100 cherry blossom spots list, three are in Kyoto (Arashiyama, Daigoji, Ninnaji).

Eastern Kyoto is particularly popular during the cherry blossom season. A walk from Nanzen-ji to Ginkaku-ji along the Philosopher's Path, lined with cherry trees, is enjoyable, as there are a variety of temples and shrines to stop at along the way. The garden of the Heian Shrine, not far from the Philosopher's Path, features colorful pink blossoms, which is a nice contrast to the white blossoms you'll see on the Philosopher's Path. The famous cherry tree in Maruyama Park is often the center of attention in the evenings when it is lit up. Vendors line the pathway leading up to it, creating a festive atmosphere. Kiyomizu-dera and Kodai-ji have extended hours during the first few days of this season offering visitors the opportunity to view them at night, lit up against the blossoms. Blossoms can also be seen along the Kamogawa River. The entire area literally blossoms in the spring!

In Central Kyoto the northern section of the Imperial Park is home to a variety of different types of cherry blossoms. Nijo Castle hosts its own Nijo Light-Up, in which visitors can walk the grounds of the castle at night among the cherry blossoms (typically for 10-14 days). You cannot enter the castle during the light-up, so those who want to enter should visit during the day to see the castle and the blossoms. Just south of Kyoto station, the grounds of Toji Temple bloom beautifully below the towering pagoda.

In Arashiyama, a large portion of the mountainside is bright with cherry blossoms, along with the area around Hankyu Arashiyama Station. During the day, many people enjoy viewing the blossoms on the mountainside from the "Romantic Train" that travels through Arashiyama. At night, the area is lit up and food stalls are set up with a variety of delicious snacks.

Northern Kyoto offers cherry-blossom scouts worthwhile experiences at Hirano Shrine and Kyoto Botanical Gardens, and a walk inside the large grounds of Daigo-ji in Southern Kyoto is certainly made memorable when all the blossoms are in full bloom.

Plum blossoms

Although they are less well-known to foreign tourists, who tend only to focus their attentions on seeing cherry blossoms, for those with plans to visit Kyoto from mid-February through mid-March, plum blossom viewing makes for a great alternative. Kyoto has two popular plum blossom locations; Kitano Tenmangu and the Kyoto Botanical Gardens, both in northern Kyoto. Kitano Tenmangu has a large grove of plum trees just outside the shrine entrance that, with a ¥600 fee, you can stroll about. Within the shrine grounds, there are many more trees (viewable for free). The shrine even hosts annual performances by geisha amidst the plum blossoms. Plum blossoms have a very pleasantly distinct fragrance. These Japanese ume trees are actually more closely related to apricot trees. However an early mistranslation by the Japanese resulted in these trees being called "plum" trees instead.

Festivals and Events

Setsubun (February 3 or 4) A large bonfire and Shinto ceremony is held at Yoshida Shrine.

Hanatoro (March 14-23 in Higashiyama and December 14-23 in Arashiyama) Streets and temples are decorated with lanterns and flowers, and many places have extended viewing hours into the night.

Cherry Blossom Season (April 1-15; days vary depending upon the weather) Although viewing the blossoms is enough for many, special events are often held throughout the city. (See "Cherry Blossoms" above)

Aoi Matsuri (May 15) Beginning at Kyoto Imperial palace, a large procession dressed in Heian Period garbs walks to Shimogamo Shrine and finishes at Kamigamo Shrine.

Gion Matsuri (July 17) Many Mikoshi are paraded through the streets. It is considered to be one of the **top three festivals** in Japan.

<u>Daimonji Gozan Okuribi</u> (August 16) The hillside in Northwestern Kyoto is lit aflame in this festival honoring one's ancestors. Candle lanterns are floated out in Hirosawa Pond.

<u>Jidai Matsuri</u> (October 22) People dressed in traditional garbs parade to Heian Shrine.

Cooking Classes

Cookly Afternoon Cooking Traditional Izakaya Dishes, Funayacho 679, Shimogyo-ku, Kyoto 600-8466 +81-75-746-5094. 2:00 pm. Afternoon Izakaya Class is a great way to immerse yourself in Japanese dining culture as well as learn authentic and popular Japanese foods that are eaten at home and in local restaurants. The course consists of two parts. First, you will cook 2-3 dishes and enjoy them. Then you will return to the kitchen and learn 2-3 more dishes before eating once more. Enjoy cooking and eating a variety of dishes in cozy atmosphere just like in Izakaya restaurants. Book online or call for reservations. Advance booking recommended due to small class sizes. ¥ 7,800.

Buying

There is a nice selection of reassuringly non-tacky traditional souvenir shops around Arashiyama station in Western Kyoto, selling fans and traditional sweets. More tacky stores can be found in Gion and the approach to Kiyomizu Temple, selling keyrings, cuddly toys, and garish ornaments. Other traditional souvenirs from Kyoto include parasols and carved wooden dolls.

More unconventional but colorful (and relatively cheap) souvenirs are the wooden votive tablets produced by Shinto shrines, which bear an image relevant to the shrine on the reverse. Visitors write their prayers on the tablets and hang them up, but there's no rule that says you can't take it with you.

Manga and anime enthusiasts should visit Teramachi Street, a covered shopping street off the main Shijo-dori, which boasts a large manga store on two floors, as well as a two-story branch of Gamers (a chain of anime stores), and a small two-story anime and collectables store.

Many ATMs in Kyoto do not allow non-domestic cr cards to be used, but ATMs in post offices and Seven-Eleven usually do. So if you find your card rejected or invalid in an ATM then try and get to a post office JP (in orange letters)) to use their ATMs instead. Look for the PLUS or Cirrus logos, whichever you find printed on the back of your ATM card. Another option is Citibank, which should work, too. There is an old standby international ATM at the top floor of Takashimaya Department Store at Shijo/Kawaramachi in the "Cash Corner." The bank of ATMs in the basement of the Kyoto Tower shopping center (across the street from JR Kyoto Station) also includes one machine where international cards may be used.

Splurge

In the shopping areas adjacent to Kiyomizudera (on the other side of the Kamo River), it is possible to purchase samurai swords and top of the line kimonos. Do not be surprised if the prices for either item exceed ¥3,000,000.

Kyoto incense is also famous. It usually has a very delicate yet fragrant bouquet. Incense is relatively agreeable in price (¥400-2000). You will be able to find it between Nishi and Higashi Hongwanji.

Damascene

Damascene, a special metal created by imbedding other metals, originated in Damascus, Syria over 2000 years ago and was first introduced to Japan in the 8th century. Since then, it has ceased production worldwide with the exception of Kyoto city, which continues producing it even today. The technique used to create Kyoto's damascene is quite complex, as it must be corroded, rusted, and boiled in tea, along with inlaying many layers of metal to produce the final product. Today, visitors can purchase a variety of jewelry, as well as vases, tea utensils, lighters, and other accessories made using this technique.

Eating

If you've just stepped off the train and the first thing on your mind is a bite to eat, there are several restaurants on the tenth and eleventh floors of the Isetan department store attached to Kyoto station. Most of the offerings are Japanese, including a veritable Ramen village, with a few casual Italian cafes as well.

Matcha

Kyoto, and the nearby city of Uji, is well known for its *matcha* or green tea, but visitors don't just come to *drink* the tea; there are a wide variety of matcha-flavored treats. Matcha ice cream is particularly popular, and most places selling ice cream will have it as an option. It also shows up in a variety of snacks and gifts.

There is one shop in Kyoto called "Maccha House" which you should really go. This is a shop which specializes in Matcha. So people can enjoy eating or drinking the original Matcha drinks and sweets which you can only eat it here in Japan. The most popular sweet in this shop is Matcha tiramisu, made out of

Matcha and a type of cheese called mascarpone. It doesn't taste so sweet, so this sweet is recommended also for people who don't like very sweet things. But not only the taste, but also the appearence looks very attractive

Yatsuhashi

Yatsuhashi is another delicious Kyoto snack. There are two types of yatsuhashi; baked and raw. The hard yatsuhashi was originally made using cinnamon, and tastes like a crunchy biscuit. Today, while the biscuits remain the same, you can also buy hard yatsuhashi dipped in *macha* and strawberry-flavored glazes.

Raw yatsuhashi, also known as *hijiri* was also made with cinnamon, but the cinnamon is mixed with bean paste and then folded into the *hijiri* to make a triangle-shape. Today, you can buy a wide variety of flavors, including *macha*, chocolate and banana, and black poppyseed. Many of the flavors are seasonal, such as the *sakura* (cherry blossom) yatsuhashi available in the spring and mango, peach, blueberry, and strawberry, available from May to October.

Although yatsuhashi can be purchased at most souvenir shops, the best place to purchase raw yatsuhashi is the famous Honkenishio Yatsuhashi. While other stores may carry yatsuhashi, this is the place to find all of the seasonal flavors, as well as free samples. Most of these shops are located in Higashiyama. The most convenient for tourists is probably the one on Kiyomizu-zaka, just below the entrance to Kiyomizu-dera.

While many tourists find raw yatsuhashi to be a delicious (and highly affordable) souvenir, be aware that it only lasts for one week after purchase. Baked yatsuhashi on the other hand, will last for about three months. Consider this when deciding what gifts to take home with you.

Mont Blanc aux Marrons (Chestnut cake)
This is one of the famous sweet which you can eat it in Kyoto, in the cafe called "Sweets Cafe Kyoto Keizo".

The special thing about this cake is that it is made by baking the meringue at a low temperature. Therefore, unlike the other cakes, this chestnut cake is said to only last for 10 minutes. This is because after 10 minutes, the texture and the taste of this cake changes dramatically. The texture and the taste of this cake changes so much that some people think they are eating a completely different cake after 10 minutes have passed.

Other specialties

Other Kyoto specialities include hamo (a white fish served with ume as sushi), tofu (try places around Nanzenji temple), suppon (an expensive turtle dish), vegetarian dishes (thanks to the abundance of temples), and kaiseki-ryori (multi-course chef's choice that can be extremely good and expensive).

Drinking

Kyoto's night scene is dominated by bars catering for local needs, most of which are located in Central

Kyotoaround Kiyamachi, between Shijo and Sanjo. This area offers a wide variety of drinking options for all types of people. You'll also have no trouble finding the host and hostess bars, courtesy of the staff pacing around out front trying to entice visitors. There are plenty of options beyond this street in other regions, but with such a large concentration of bars along in the same area, its easy to locate a place where you feel most at home to relax for the night.

If you're looking for nightclubs, Kyoto has a few options, but it is not a city known for its thriving dance clubs. Those hoping to experience that part of Japanese nightlife should consider taking a train to Osaka where many of the clubs are hip and wild enough to rival any Tokyo club.

Sake

Some of Kyoto's most famous sake comes from Gekkeikan Brewery in the Fushimi area of Southern Kyoto. A 400 year old brewery that still produces great sake, Gekkeikan offers tours of its facilities.

Sleep

This guide uses the following price ranges for a standard *double* room:	
Budget	below ¥11,000
Mid-range	¥11,000–20,000
Splurge	over ¥20,000

Kyoto has a wide range of accommodation, much of it geared towards foreign visitors. During peak seasons, such as the cherry blossoms in April or during Golden Week when accommodation is difficult to get, consider staying in Osaka. A thirty minute train ride from Kyoto Station to Osaka Station will cost you ¥540 one way. Since Kyoto is a major tourist destination, demand is high and prices follow suit.

Most of the lodging in the city is clustered near the central city, especially around Kyoto Station and the downtown area near Karasuma-Oike. The outer areas have a scattering of their own, tending towards inexpensive but often much further from train or subway stations.

Budget

At the bottom of the price scale, many temples in Kyoto own and run their own lodging complex known as *shukubō*, usually located on or near temple grounds. Guests are often invited to participate in morning prayer service (*otsutome*) held at the temple. Unfortunately, most temple lodgings do not have English-speaking receptions, and curfews and check-in/out times tend to be strict. Most are located in the northern region of the city.

Hostels are common and popular with students. Inexpensive hotels lack amenities but compensate with prices surprisingly low for Japan; both can be found in all regions of the city, and may be the only options available if you need to stay in an outlying ward.

The majority of self-named ryokan in this range are actually minshuku. Most are small family-run operations and accustomed to dealing with foreigners. Be prepared to pay for the full stay in advance.

As in other Japanese cities, internet cafes and capsule hotels are available for those truly on the cheap. Expect to pay around ¥2000 for a night's stay in an internet cafe. You get a computer, a comfortable chair, and all the tea and hot chocolate you want.

For long-term stay, JamHouses near Nijō Castle and Katsura station offer inexpensive shared houses with Japanese roommates. Houses have private rooms and dormitories, equipped kitchens and living rooms. JamHouse near Nijō Castle has also a restaurant.

Internet and manga cafés
These "manga-kisas" (short for kissaten which means 'cafe') are not a thing to fear. There is nothing wrong with staying in these Japan#Last_resorts for a few nights. Most manga-kisas have no separate smoking and non-smoking sections, and the bountiful collections of manga will only be in japanese, but they usually have cushions and blankets and free unlimited

soft drinks (included with entry fee). Showers are usually available, but sometimes for a fee. Remember that these cafés won't keep your luggage during the day so either keep it with you, find free storage elsewhere or use a coin locker (¥300-600 per use). The price will usually not be that different from a normal hotel for an overnight stay.

Topscafé, Hachijo street (south-east of Kyoto JR station, 5min by walk, near willerexpress bus stop), Cost is: 120or140 / 1000 / 1800 / 3000 / 1500 + member card 200 + vip: +200 for pack + 100y/15min overtime night starts at 1500y+member card. internet hour starts at 480+member card.

every 15min (single or vip)	3h pack	6h pack	12h pack	night pack 7h
120or140	1000	1800	3000	1500

Freespace, south of Shin-kyogoku, near Sanjo-Kawaramachi. cost: member card 200, towel rent 210 open area has a variety of seat: normal, reclining, massage but can't be reserved. It allows even you take the cheap price to have a comfortable seat. night starts at 980y+member card. internet hour starts at 480+member card.

	30mn	15mn extra	4h	7h	6h (night)	8h (night)	12h
open	240	100	980	1280	980	-	1500
vip	280	100	1150	1600	1280	1580	1980

<u>Popeye media cafe</u>, (between kyoto shiyakusho-mae station/honno-ji and sanjo-dori, just near catholic cathedral and Royal Hotel and spa, bus stop kawaramachi-sanjo 4/17/205),. The most famous one. Cafetaria seat are ok but better to use two if sleeping. no member card, shower extra 100y if cafetaria (included in other case), 100y for towel rent no member card. night starts at 880/1100y. internet hour starts at 280.

Kyoto City Travel Guide, Japan

	1h first charge	15min after	3h pack (day)	6h (day)	5h (night)	10h (night)
cafetaria (unreserved seat, normally only free drinks+manga, NO internet/wifi normally)	280	70	680	1180	880	1100
open seat (+games+dvd)	420	95	920	1480	980	1230
business (+tv)	470	115	1020	1780	1280	1980
reclining	525	125	1230	2180	1550	3100
massage or pair-sofa or flat	525	125	1230	2180	1760	3520

Midrange

The boundary between budget and midrange is often unclear, particularly among ryokan. Hotels in this category are concentrated in Central Kyoto, serving the business market with the typical amenities and close proximity to transportation. There are also a number of smaller, family-run guesthouses around the Gojo area, which is between Kyoto Station area and historical Gion.

Splurge
Split between the downtown and Higashiyama areas on each side of the Kamogawa River, these top-of-the-line lodgings can make your airfare look cheap. Western-style hotels dominate in this category; unlike the midrange options, very few of the high end ryokan can be booked without a fluent command of Japanese.

Machiya-stay
In Kyoto, there are traditional wooden townhouses called Kyo-Machiya or Machiya. Kyo-Machiya defined the architectural atmosphere of downtown Kyoto for centuries, and represents the standard defining form of Machiya throughout the country.

There are several facilities offers those Machiya to the travellers to stay privately, and can experience the traditional living in Kyoto. Most of those facilities are located in central Kyoto that easy to access to any sightseeing spot. However, generally those facilities don't offer any meals, but in Kyoto, there is a delivery system from the Japanese restaurant that customer can order and eat in the Kyo-Machiya. During the guest stay, it is completely private that guests can feel like staying at their home.

The size of the facilities are average 80m^2, can stay from 2 people with prices comperable to a mid range hotel (¥10,000 per night) but it can be better to use with a group of 4 to 6, or with family. There are facilities that guests can stay together in the same Machiya for up to 14 people.

The price is from ¥25,000-

Getting out

Asuka - the cradle of Japanese civilization. The first Japanese Emperors established the capital here, and the oldest shrines, tombs, and temples are in Asuka.

<u>Uji</u> - the best tea in Japan and the Byodo-in temple.

<u>Kurama</u> - less than an hour's journey by a local train from Kyoto Demachi-Yanagi station, the small village of Kurama has real *onsen* (Japanese natural hot springs). A nice mountain walk can be made to Kibune, where you can take the train back to Kyoto. The trail is broad and not dangerous, but it consists of many steps. The trip would take 90 minutes (if you don't look too long to all temples and shrines along the route). A map can be obtained from tourist information in Kyoto station.

<u>Lake Biwa</u> - if the summer humidity has drained your will to sightsee, take a day swimming at the underrated beaches of western Lake Biwa. Popular choices include Omi Maiko and Shiga Beach, each about 40 minutes from Kyoto on the JR Kosei Line.

<u>Mount Hiei</u> - an ancient hilltop temple complex that traditionally guarded (and occasionally raided) Kyoto.

<u>Otsu</u> - home to some great historical temples, Mount Hiei, and one of Lake Biwa's ports.

Koka - home of ninjas, and there is the Miho Museum.

Nara - less than an hour's journey by train on the JR Nara line from Kyoto station, Nara is an even older capital than Kyoto and has a stunning collection of temples in a giant landscaped park.

Osaka - about half an hour from Kyoto by JR rapid train, this bustling city offers more retail opportunities and a central castle.

Amanohashidate - literally "the bridge to heaven", it is considered one of Japan's top three scenic views (along with Matsushima in Miyagi prefectureand Miyajima in Hiroshima prefecture). It forms a thin strip of land straddling the Miyazu Bay in northern Kyoto Prefecture, hence the name. Visitors are asked to turn their backs toward the view, bend over, and look at it between their legs.

Himeji - about an hour by Shinkansen west of Kyoto, Himeji boasts a spectacular traditional castle.

Attractions

Enryaku-ji

Located atop 848m-high Hiei-zan (the mountain that dominates the skyline in the northeast of the city), the Enryaku-ji complex is an entire world of temples and dark forests that feels a long way from the hustle and bustle of the city below. A visit here is a good way to spend half a day hiking, poking around temples and enjoying the atmosphere of a key site in Japanese history. There are some incredible views of the mountains and Biwa-ko (Lake Biwa).

Enryaku-ji was founded in 788 by Saichō, also known as Dengyō-daishi, the priest who established the Tenzai school. This school did not receive imperial recognition until 823, after Saichō's death; however, from the 8th century the temple grew in power. At its height, Enryaku-ji possessed some 3000 buildings and an army of thousands of *sōhei* (warrior monks). In 1571 Oda Nobunaga saw the temple's power as a threat to his aims to unify the nation and he destroyed most of the buildings, along with the monks inside. Today only three pagodas and 120 minor temples remain.

The complex is divided into three sections: Tōtō, Saitō and Yokawa. The Tōtō (eastern pagoda section) contains the Kompon Chū-dō (Primary Central Hall), which is the most important building in the complex. The flames on the three dharma lamps in front of the altar have been kept lit for more than 1200 years. The Daikō-dō (Great Lecture Hall) displays life-sized wooden statues of the founders of various Buddhist schools. This part of the temple is heavily geared to group access, with large expanses of asphalt for parking.

The Saitō (western pagoda section) contains the Shaka-dō, which dates from 1595 and houses a rare Buddha sculpture of the Shaka Nyorai (Historical Buddha). The Saitō, with its stone paths winding through forests of tall trees, temples shrouded in mist and the sound of distant gongs, is the most atmospheric part of the temple. Hold on to your ticket from the Tōtō section, as you may need to show it here.

The Yokawa is of minimal interest and a 4km bus ride away from the Saitō area. The Chū-dō here was originally built in 848. It was destroyed by fire several times and has undergone repeated reconstruction (most recently in 1971). If you plan to visit this area as well as Tōtō and Saitō, allow a full day for in-depth exploration.

You can reach Hiei-zan and Enryaku-ji by train or bus. The most interesting way is the train/cable-car/funicular route starting on the Eizan line from Demachiyanagi Station to Yase Hieizanguchi. Note that this cable-car/funicular route does not operate in winter from early December to mid-March. You can also access Enryaku-ji by the JR Kosei line from Kyoto Station to Heizan Sakamoto Station and then a bus to the Sakamoto cable-car station, which runs year-round. If you're in a hurry or would like to save money, the best way is a direct bus from Sanjō Keihan or Kyoto stations.

Note that the Japanese word for funicular is *ropeway*. From the funicular station, you can hike through the wooded forest (2.2km) to the Tōtō section. Otherwise, it's a short walk to the bus station, from where you can board a bus to the Enryaku-ji Bus Center for the Tōtō section. You can hike between all three sections; otherwise the bus runs between them all quite frequently.

There's a simple canteen in the Enryaku-ji Bus Center serving noodle dishes.

Kiyomizu-dera

A buzzing hive of activity perched on a hill overlooking the basin of Kyoto, Kiyomizu-dera is one of Kyoto's most popular and most enjoyable temples. It may not be a tranquil refuge, but it represents the favoured expression of faith in Japan. The excellent site is a great first port of call for information on the temple, plus a how-to guide to praying here. Note that the Main Hall is undergoing renovations and may be covered, but is still accessible.

This ancient temple was first built in 798, but the present buildings are reconstructions dating from 1633. As an affiliate of the Hossō school of Buddhism, which originated in Nara, it has successfully survived the many intrigues of local Kyoto schools of Buddhism through the centuries and is now one of the most famous landmarks of the city (for which reason it can get very crowded during spring and autumn).

The Hondō (Main Hall) has a huge verandah that is supported by pillars and juts out over the hillside. Just below this hall is the waterfall Otowa-no-taki, where visitors drink sacred waters believed to bestow health and longevity. Dotted around the precincts are other halls and shrines. At Jishu-jinja, the shrine up the steps above the main hall, visitors try to ensure success in love by closing their eyes and walking about 18m between a pair of stones – if you miss the stone, your desire for love won't be fulfilled! Note that you can ask someone to guide you, but if you do, you'll need someone's assistance to find your true love.

Before you enter the actual temple precincts, check out the Tainai-meguri, the entrance to which is just to the left (north) of the pagoda that is located in front of the main entrance to the temple (¥100 donation; open 9am to 4pm). We won't tell you too much about it as it will ruin the experience. Suffice to say that by entering the Tainai-meguri, you are symbolically entering the womb of a female bodhisattva. When you get to the rock in the darkness, spin it in either direction to make a wish.

The steep approach to the temple is known as Chawan-zaka (Teapot Lane) and is lined with shops selling Kyoto handicrafts, local snacks and souvenirs.

.

Fushimi Inari-Taisha

With seemingly endless arcades of vermilion *torii* (shrine gates) spread across a thickly wooded mountain, this vast shrine complex is a world unto its own. It is, quite simply, one of the most impressive and memorable sights in all of Kyoto.

The entire complex, consisting of five shrines, sprawls across the wooded slopes of Inari-san. A pathway wanders 4km up the mountain and is lined with dozens of atmospheric sub-shrines.

Fushimi Inari was dedicated to the gods of rice and sake by the Hata family in the 8th century. As the role of agriculture diminished, deities were enrolled to ensure prosperity in business. Nowadays, the shrine is one of Japan's most popular, and is the head shrine for some 40,000 Inari shrines scattered the length and breadth of the country.

As you explore the shrine, you will come across hundreds of stone foxes. The fox is considered the messenger of Inari, the god of cereals, and the stone foxes, too, are often referred to as Inari. The key often seen in the fox's mouth is for the rice granary. On an incidental note, the Japanese traditionally see the fox as a sacred, somewhat mysterious figure capable of 'possessing' humans – the favoured point of entry is under the fingernails.

The walk around the upper precincts of the shrine is a pleasant day hike. It also makes for a very eerie stroll in the late afternoon and early evening, when the various graveyards and miniature shrines along the path take on a mysterious air. It's best to go with a friend at this time.

On 8 April there's a Sangyō-sai festival with offerings and dances to ensure prosperity for national industry. During the first few days in January, thousands of believers visit this shrine as their *hatsu-mōde* (first shrine visit of the New Year) to pray for good fortune. For info on the shrine's many schedules, see http://inari.jp/en/rite.

Chion-in

A collection of soaring buildings, spacious courtyards and gardens, Chion-in serves as the headquarters of the Jōdo sect, the largest school of Buddhism in Japan. It's the most popular pilgrimage temple in Kyoto and it's always a hive of activity. For visitors with a taste for the grand, this temple is sure to satisfy.

Chion-in was established in 1234 on the site where Hōnen, one of the most famous figures in Japanese Buddhism, taught his brand of Buddhism (Jōdo, or Pure Land, Buddhism) and eventually fasted to death.

The oldest of the present buildings date to the 17th century. The two-storey San-mon temple gate is the largest in Japan. The immense Miei-dō Hall (Main Hall) contains an image of Hōnen. It's connected to another hall, the Dai Hōjō, by a 'nightingale' floor (that sings and squeaks at every move, making it difficult for intruders to move about quietly). Miei-dō Hall is currently under restoration and closed to the public. It's expected to be finished by 2020.

Up a flight of steps southeast of the main hall is the temple's giant bell, which was cast in 1633 and weighs 70 tonnes. It is the largest bell in Japan. The bell is rung by the temple's monks 108 times on New Year's Eve each year.

The temple has two gardens – the Hōjō garden designed around a pond in the *chisen kaiyūshiki* style, and the Yuzen-en featuring a *karesansui*(dry rock garden).

Tōfuku-ji

Home to a spectacular garden, several superb structures and beautiful precincts, Tōfuku-ji is one of the best temples in Kyoto. It's well worth a visit and can easily be paired with a trip to Fushimi Inari-Taisha (the temples are linked by the Keihan and JR train lines). The present temple complex includes 24 subtemples. The huge San-mon is the oldest Zen main gate in Japan, the Hōjō (Abbot's Hall) was reconstructed in 1890, and the gardens were laid out in 1938.

The northern garden has stones and moss neatly arranged in a chequerboard pattern. From a viewing platform at the back of the gardens you can observe the Tsūten-kyō (Bridge to Heaven), which spans a valley filled with maples.

Founded in 1236 by the priest Enni, Tōfuku-ji belongs to the Rinzai sect of Zen Buddhism. As this temple was intended to compare with Tōdai-ji and Kōfuku-ji in Nara, it was given a name combining characters from the names of each of these temples.

Tōfuku-ji offers regular Zen meditation sessions for beginners, but don't expect coddling or English-language explanations: this is the real deal. Get a Japanese speaker to enquire at the temple about the next session (it holds about four a month for beginners).

Note that Tōfuku-ji is one of Kyoto's most famous autumn-foliage spots, and it is invariably packed during the peak of colours in November. Otherwise, it's often very quiet.

Gion

Gion is the famous entertainment and geisha quarter on the eastern bank of the Kamo-gawa. While Gion's true origins were in teahouses catering to weary visitors to the nearby shrine Yasaka-jinja, by the mid-18th century the area was Kyoto's largest pleasure district. The best way to experience Gion today is with an evening stroll around the atmospheric streets lined with 17th-century traditional restaurants and teahouses lit up with lanterns. Start off on the main street Hanami-kōji, which runs north–south and bisects Shijō-dōri.

At the southern section of Hanami-kōji, many of the restaurants and teahouses are exclusive establishments for geisha entertainment. At the south end you reach Gion Corner and Gion Kōbu Kaburen-jō Theatre.

If you walk from Shijō-dōri along the northern section of Hanami-kōji and take your third left, you will find yourself on Shimbashi (sometimes called Shirakawa Minami-dōri), which is one of Kyoto's most beautiful streets, especially in the evening and during cherry-blossom season. A bit further north lie Shinmonzen-dōri and Furumonzen-dōri, running east–west. Wander in either direction along these streets, which are packed with old houses, art galleries and shops specialising in antiques – but don't expect flea-market prices.

Nijō-jō

The military might of Japan's great warlord generals, the Tokugawa shoguns, is amply demonstrated by the imposing stone walls and ramparts of their great castle, Nijō-jō, which dominates a large part of Northwest Kyoto. Hidden behind these you will find a superb palace surrounded by beautiful gardens. As you might expect, a sight of this grandeur attracts a lot of crowds, so it's best to visit just after opening or shortly before closing.

This castle was built in 1603 as the official Kyoto residence of the first Tokugawa shogun, Ieyasu. The ostentatious style of its construction was intended as a demonstration of Ieyasu's prestige and also to signal the demise of the emperor's power. As a safeguard against treachery, Ieyasu had the interior fitted with 'nightingale' floors, as well as concealed chambers where bodyguards could keep watch.

After passing through the grand Kara-mon gate, you enter Ninomarupalace, which is divided into five buildings with numerous chambers. The Ōhiroma Yon-no-Ma (Fourth Chamber) has spectacular screen paintings. Don't miss the excellent Ninomaru Palace Garden, which was designed by the tea master and landscape architect Kobori Enshū.

Audio guides are available (¥500) and English guided tours run daily at 10.30am and 12.30pm (¥2000, not including entry price).

Daitoku-ji

For anyone with the slightest fondness for Japanese gardens, don't miss this network of lanes dotted with atmospheric Zen temples. Daitoku-ji, the main temple here, serves as headquarters for the Rinzai Daitoku-ji school of Zen Buddhism. It's not usually open to the public but there are several subtemples with superb carefully raked *karen-sensui* (dry landscape) garden well worth making the trip out for. Highlights among the subtemples open to the public include Daisen-in, Kōtō-in, Ryōgen-in and Zuihō-in.

Daitoku-ji is on the eastern side of the grounds. It was founded in 1319, burnt down in the next century and rebuilt in the 16th century. The San-mon gate (1589) has a self-carved statue of its erector, the famous tea master Sen no Rikyū, on its 2nd storey.

The Karasuma subway line to Kitaōji Station is the fastest way to get here. From Kitaōji Station, walk west along Kitaōji-dōri for about 15 minutes. You'll see the temple complex on your right. The main entrance is a bit north of Kitaōji. If you enter from the main gate, which is on the east side of the complex, you'll soon find Daitoku-ji on your right. Alternatively, take bus 205 or 206 from Kyoto Station to the Daitokuji-mae bus stop.

Eikan-dō

Perhaps Kyoto's most famous (and most crowded) autumn-foliage destination, Eikan-dō is a superb temple just a short walk south of the famous Path of Philosophy. Eikan-dō is made interesting by its varied architecture, its gardens and its works of art. It was founded as Zenrin-ji in 855 by the priest Shinshō, but the name was changed to Eikan-dō in the 11th century to honour the philanthropic priest Eikan.

In the Amida-dō hall at the southern end of the complex is a famous statue of Mikaeri Amida Buddha glancing backwards.

From Amida-dō, head north to the end of the curving covered garyūrō(walkway). Change into the sandals provided, then climb the steep steps up the mountainside to the Tahō-tō pagoda, from where there's a fine view across the city.

For most of November, when the autumn leaves are at their best, the admission fee increases to ¥1000 during the day, and the temple stays open to 9pm for the nighttime illumination (¥600).

Ginkaku-ji

Home to a sumptuous garden and elegant structures, Ginkaku-ji is one of Kyoto's premier sites. The temple started its life in 1482 as a retirement villa for Shogun Ashikaga Yoshimasa, who desired a place to retreat from the turmoil of a civil war. While the name Ginkaku-ji literally translates as 'Silver Pavilion', the shogun's ambition to cover the building with silver was never realised. After Yoshimasa's death, the villa was converted into a temple.

Walkways lead through the gardens, which include meticulously raked cones of white sand (said to be symbolic of a mountain and a lake), tall pines and a pond in front of the temple. A path also leads up the mountainside through the trees.

Note that Ginkaku-ji is one of the city's most popular sites, and it is almost always crowded, especially during spring and autumn. We strongly recommend visiting right after it opens or just before it closes.

Nanzen-ji

This is one of the most rewarding temples in Kyoto, with its expansive grounds and numerous subtemples. At its entrance stands the massive San-mon. Steps lead up to the 2nd storey, which has a great view over the city. Beyond the gate is the main hall of the temple, above which you will find the Hōjō, where the Leaping Tiger Garden is a classic Zen garden well worth a look.

Nanzen-ji began as a retirement villa for Emperor Kameyama but was dedicated as a Zen temple on his death in 1291. Civil war in the 15th century destroyed most of the temple; the present buildings date from the 17th century. It operates now as headquarters for the Rinzai school of Zen.

While you're in the Hōjō, you can enjoy a cup of *matcha* (powdered green tea) and a sweet while gazing at a small waterfall (¥500; ask at the reception desk of the Hōjō).

Tenryū-ji

A major temple of the Rinzai school, Tenryū-ji has one of the most attractive gardens in all of Kyoto, particularly during the spring cherry-blossom and autumn-foliage seasons. The main 14th-century Zen garden, with its backdrop of the Arashiyama mountains, is a good example of *shakkei* (borrowed scenery). Unfortunately, it's no secret that the garden here is world class, so it pays to visit early in the morning or on a weekday.

It was built in 1339 on the old site of Go-Daigo's villa after a priest had a dream of a dragon rising from the nearby river. The dream was seen as a sign that the emperor's spirit was uneasy and so the temple was built as appeasement – hence the name *tenryū* (heavenly dragon). The present buildings date from 1900. You will find Arashiyama's famous bamboo grove situated just outside the north gate of the temple.

Shōren-in

This temple is hard to miss, with its giant camphor trees growing just outside the walls. Fortunately, most tourists march right on past, heading to the area's more famous temples. That is their loss, because this intimate little sanctuary contains a superb landscape garden, which you can enjoy while drinking a cup of green tea (¥500; ask at the reception office, not available in summer).

Shōren-in, commonly called Awata Palace after the neighbourhood in which it is located, was originally the residence of the chief abbot of the Tendai school. Founded in 1150, the present building dates from 1895 and the main hall has sliding screens with paintings from the 16th and 17th centuries.

Kinkaku-ji

Kyoto's famed 'Golden Pavilion', Kinkaku-ji is one of Japan's best-known sights. The main hall, covered in brilliant gold leaf, shining above its reflecting pond is truly spectacular. Needless to say, due to its beauty, the temple can be packed any day of the year. It's best to go early in the day or just before closing, ideally on a weekday.

The original building dates from 1397 and was a retirement villa for shogun Ashikaga Yoshimitsu. His son converted it into a temple. In 1950 a young monk consummated his obsession with the temple by burning it to the ground. The monk's story was fictionalised in Mishima Yukio's *The Temple of the Golden Pavilion*. In 1955 a full reconstruction was completed that followed the original design, but the gold-foil covering was extended to the lower floors.

Aritsugu

While you're in Nishiki Market, have a look at this store – it has some of the best kitchen knives in the world. Choose your knife – all-rounder, sushi, vegetable – and the staff will show you how to care for it before sharpening and boxing it up. You can also have your name engraved in English or Japanese. Knives start at around ¥10,000.

Founded in 1560, Aritsugu was originally involved in the production of swords and the blacksmith skills have been passed down over the years through generation after generation. It also carries a selection of excellent and unique Japanese kitchenware and whetstones for knife sharpening.

Kanei

A small traditional place not far from Funaoka Onsen, Kanei is for soba (buckwheat noodles) connoisseurs – the noodles are made by hand and are delicious. The owners don't speak much English, so here's what to order: *zaru soba* (cold soba; ¥950) or *kake soba* (soba in a broth; ¥1000). Prepare to queue and note that noodles often sell out early.

Note that handmade soba quickly loses its taste and texture, so it's recommend that you eat it quickly. The servings are small and the dishes are only likely to please real soba fans. Kanei is on the corner, a few metres west of Sarasa Nishijin.

Giro Giro Hitoshina

Giro Giro takes traditional *kaiseki* (Japanese haute cuisine) and strips any formality so you're left with great food but in a boisterous atmosphere and with thousands more yen left in your pocket. In a quiet lane near Kiyamachi-dōri, things liven up inside with patrons sitting at the counter around the open kitchen chatting it up with chefs preparing inventive dishes.

The seasonal menu consists of eight courses. There are upstairs tables, too, but if you want a counter seat, book well in advance; for a Friday or Saturday night you'll need to allow a couple of months in advance. Cash only.

The End

www.ingramcontent.com/pod-product-compliance
Lightning Source LLC
Chambersburg PA
CBHW031103080526
44587CB00011B/800